THE
GRAMMAR
REFERENCE GUIDE

2nd Edition

division of PARK University Enterprises, Inc.

9757 Metcalf Avenue • Overland Park, KS 66212
Phone: (800) 556-3009 • Fax: (913) 967-8847
www.careertrack.com

The Grammar Reference Guide - 2nd Edition
ISBN 1-933328-54-1 Item #34002

Printed in the United States of America

For more information about *The Grammar Reference Guide* or other products available from
CareerTrack, contact 800-556-3009 or visit us at www.careertrack.com.

TABLE OF CONTENTS

TABLE OF CONTENTS

TABLE OF CONTENTS

TABLE OF CONTENTS

INTRODUCTION

The Grammar Reference Guide is created for individuals who want to speak and write well and who can't afford to have grammatical and spelling errors tarnish their image. The guide is easy to use and contains answers for the most frequently asked grammar questions.

This book can be used as a self-instruction guide, and is defined in short "bites," which makes it perfect for reading at your desk, on a break, or while waiting in the dentist's office. Once you read this book, you will find that you can utilize it in many ways.

When you are composing a letter, memo, or report, and come across something that is unclear, this handy reference guide will be the first thing you want to reach for to clear up your questions.

This guide fits nicely on your shelf next to your dictionary and thesaurus and serves as a perfect resource that you need at your fingertips. Use the table of contents and index to quickly and easily reference anything you need.

Build credibility
By using this guide to understand the finer points of language and grammatical rules, you are cleaning up not only your writing, but also your overall image, and how readers will view you. When the reader doesn't have to wade through grammatical errors, they can focus on the content of your writing, and you will look more credible and can get your message across in a clear and concise manner.

Test your knowledge
Yes, you can pop quiz yourself anytime you desire! Helpful exercises are located at the back of the guide, and give you an opportunity to review and test your knowledge on everything from spelling to sentence structure. Practice makes perfect. By testing yourself on these finer points of grammar, you can help ensure that you will recognize those same instances in your writing.

Tell your friends
How many times has a colleague shouted over to your desk, asking you the correct spelling of a word, or if you should use "who" or "whom"? Or worse, how many times have you reviewed a colleague's writing only to notice there are several errors that could have been avoided if they had taken the time to look up the proper grammatical rule? Now, you can share this guide with them. After familiarizing yourself with this guide, you can express your expert knowledge of the grammar world and guide others to this helpful at-your-fingertips reference tool.

WRITING EFFECTIVE SENTENCES

Effective writing emphasizes important information and ideas in sentences by making them obvious to the reader.

Ways to emphasize ideas

✔ Put important ideas at the beginning or ending of a sentence.

> Education remains, in spite of its shortcomings, the most important single means of economic advancement.

✔ Arrange items logically in order of either increasing or decreasing importance.

> The hurricane knocked down several trees in town, tore the roofs of several buildings, and killed nine people.
>
> Increased efficiency, a larger sales force, and improved products—these are the goals for this year.

✔ Carefully repeat key words and phrases.

> "We have the tools, all the tools—we are suffocating in tools—but we cannot find the actual wood to work or even the actual hand to work it."
> —Archibald MacLeish

✔ Set off important ideas with punctuation.

> Basketball—that is, winning basketball games—is an extremely profitable university operation.

✔ Use the active voice.

Passive:

> For energy conservation, it is urged that all lights be turned off when not in use.

Active:

> To save energy, students should turn off all lights they are not using.

✔ Write concisely.

Weak:

> In my opinion, the competition in the area of grades is distracting. It distracts many students from their goal, which is to obtain an education that is good.

Strong:

> The competition for grades distracts many students from their goal of obtaining a good education.

WRITING EFFECTIVE SENTENCES

✔ Make comparisons logical and complete.

Illogical:
> Los Angeles is larger than **any** city in California.

> *Since Los Angeles is itself a city in California, the sentence seems to say that Los Angeles is larger than itself.*

Logical:
> Los Angeles is larger than **any other** city in California.

✔ Make sure that items in a comparison or a list all have the same grammatical construction.

Faulty Parallelism:
> Formerly, accounts were submitted bi-weekly, while now they are accepted once a month.

Corrected Parallelism:
> Formerly, accounts were submitted bi-weekly; now they are submitted monthly.

Faulty Comparison:
> I like to drive my car better than my husband.

Corrected Comparison:
> I like to drive my car better than my husband's.

✔ Vary the beginnings of your sentences throughout a piece of writing.

Begin with a descriptive phrase.

💣 **Caution:** What follows the comma must be what the descriptive phrase describes.

Illogical:
> Covered in blue paint, the home-improvement accident made Eva laugh anyway.

Logical:
> Covered in blue paint, Eva laughed despite the home-improvement accident.

3

SENTENCE CONSTRUCTION

Create good sentence structure by using the acronym SVC (subject, verb, completer).

Subjects

Subjects come first to tell your reader who or what you are talking about. Subjects are nouns or pronouns. Nouns name all people, places, things, qualities, concepts, and "active" things including gerunds (actions that are things).

> People: Bill, secretary, mother, child

> Places: office, Chicago, Georgia

> Things: car, television, memo, desk

> Qualities: truthfulness, honesty, attentiveness

> Concepts: love, beauty, anger

> "Active" things: singing, running, traveling

Pronouns

A pronoun may "pinch hit" for a noun so that the same people, places, and things are not repeated over and over.

Without pronouns, this statement is awkward and redundant:

> The manager went into the manager's office to prepare the manager's report for the meeting at which the manager planned to present the manager's new budget request.

Pronouns allow a more concise and clear statement:

> The manager went into her office to prepare her report for the meeting at which she planned to present her new budget request.

💣 **Caution:** A pronoun must agree with its "antecedent" (the word for which it stands).

> *Incorrect:*

> Each of the boys liked their teacher.

> *Correct:*

> **Each** of the boys liked **his** teacher.

SENTENCE CONSTRUCTION

Pronouns that act as **subjects**:

I	we
you	they
he	who
she	it

Pronouns that act as **objects** (objects of verbs or objects of prepositions):

me	us
you	them
him	whom
her	it

Pronouns that **show ownership** (possessives):

my, mine	our, ours	its
your, yours	their, theirs	
his	her, hers	

💣 **Caution:** *Who* and *whom* should not be used interchangeably.

To figure out whether to use *who* or *whom*, replace the word with *he* or *him*. If *he* sounds right, use *who*. If *him* sounds right, use *whom*.

See also: Plural nouns and possession, *Plurals and Possessives* section

Reflexive pronouns:

her	it
myself	ourselves
yourself, yourselves	themselves
himself	itself
herself	

Reflexive pronouns are used in three main situations:
- When the subject and object are the same.
- As the object of a preposition, referring to the subject.
- When you want to emphasize the subject.

💣 **Caution:** Do not use a reflexive pronoun unless the sentence contains the noun to which it refers. For example, *myself* would only appear in a sentence containing the *I*.

Incorrect:
> Jim, Esperanza, and myself were planning a trip.

Correct:

Jim, Esperanza, and I were planning a trip.

SENTENCE CONSTRUCTION

Verbs

Verbs are the action of the sentence and tell us what is happening or taking place. You often will find more than one verb in a sentence because several different actions are taking place.

Verbs generally show action, possession, and being.

✔ **Action**
To write, to sing, to walk, to think, to run, to know.

> John **will walk** in the annual charity walk-a-thon.
>
> Mary **knows** every punctuation rule.

✔ **Possession**
To have.

> The office **has** new carpeting.
>
> Bill and Ellen **have** a home they are remodeling.

&✓**See also**: Possessives, *Plurals and Possessives* section

✔ **Being**
To be has many common forms: *am, is, are, was, were, will be, has been, had been, have been, is being, will have been.* It is often called a "linking verb" because it connects a subject to other nouns or adjectives that describe it. Nouns describing a subject are called "predicate nominatives," and adjectives describing a subject are called "predicate adjectives."

> Bill **is** nice. (Nice *is a predicate adjective.*)
>
> Arthur **will be** the fourth president to receive the Leadership Award. (President *is a predicate nominative.*)

Subject and verb agreement

Since subjects and verbs together provide the main idea or content of a sentence, they must have the right relationship, which is called "agreement." Singular subjects require singular verbs, and plural subjects require plural verbs.

> **One person** out of several hundred applicants **is to be awarded** the prize.
>
> **Several people** out of 300 applicants **are to be awarded** the prizes.

SENTENCE CONSTRUCTION

If two subjects both identify the same person or thing, the verb is singular.

> The **winner** and new "Customer Service **Representative** of the Year" **is** Ms. Trisha Carlson.
>
> **Macaroni** and **cheese is** a low-cost and healthy dinner choice.

Some words are always singular:

anyone	each	anybody	every
everyone	either	everybody	neither
someone	none	somebody	another
one	nobody		

💣 **Caution:** Two subjects joined by *or* or *nor* take a singular verb.

Incorrect:

> Either the tenant or the owner must present their grievances.

Correct:

> Either the tenant **or** the owner must present **his** grievances.

Accuracy tips for agreement

Mentally omit prepositional phrases (starting with: *in, of, for, with, by, from, to*) immediately following the subject and preceding the verb.

> **Each** (of the programmers) **has** 10 or more years of experience.
>
> **Either** (of the supervisors) **is** able to answer your question.

Ignore expressions beginning with *as well as, in addition to, accompanied by,* and other explanatory phrases. They always follow the subject and precede the verb.

> The **paper**, as well as the pens and pencils, **has been counted**.

Look to the meaning rather than the spelling to decide whether the subject is singular or plural.

> The **World Series is** almost over.
> **Economics is a** required subject.

SENTENCE CONSTRUCTION

Collective nouns

A collective noun is a singular word that refers to a number of people or things acting as a unit. While they may occasionally be plural when indicating separate actions, most collectives are singular.

> The **class** of new supervisors **is scheduled** to begin training on hiring and firing practices soon.
>
> The **committee hopes** to meet at 1 p.m.

☞ **See also**: Compound nouns and possession, *Plurals and Possessives* section

Completers

Completers finish the thoughts of subjects and verbs. An adjective or a noun may "complete" the thought begun by the subject and verb.

✔ **Objects**

Objects tell your reader what the verb is doing. They answer the questions "what or whom?" and are always nouns or pronouns.

> Linda gave the **report** to the Purchasing Department.
> *(Linda gave . . . what?)*
>
> John saw **Mary** at the meeting.
> *(John saw . . . whom?)*
>
> They questioned **Susan** about the new procedure.
> *(They questioned . . . whom?)*
>
>   S   V   C
> **Ellen completed** the **reports** before her deadline.
>
>   S   V   C
> **Chicago** usually **lives** up to its **reputation** as the "Windy City."

✔ **Predicate adjectives and nominatives**

An adjective completing the subject and verb is called a "predicate adjective," and a noun completing the subject and verb is called a "predicate nominative." They both always follow some form of the verb *to be*, often called a "linking verb" because it links the subject to the completed thought. Verbs such as *looks, seems*, and *feels* are also linking verbs when they could be replaced by *is*.

>   S V   C
> **Ellen is** very **tall**. (Tall *is a predicate adjective*.)
>
>   S V   C
> **John is** the **winner** of the "employee-of-the-month" contest. (Winner *is a predicate nominative*.)

SENTENCE CONSTRUCTION

Verb tenses

Since verbs are at the heart of sentences, let's look more closely at how they're formed. The **tense** of the verb refers to **when** something is occurring.

✔ **Present tense**

➤ An action taking place right now.

> We **are distributing** accounting reports today.

➤ An action that goes on continually.

> I **see** Mary every day.

➤ A general truth.

> Holidays **are** fun.

✔ **Past tense**

➤ An action that occurred in the past.

> I **finished** that report yesterday.

✔ **Future tense**

➤ An action that will occur in the future. *Will* is used to support the action taking place.

> Mary **will attend** the meeting on Thursday.

➤ *Shall* is used only in the following ways, and then only in formal situations:

1. When expressing future tense in the first person.

> Yes, I **shall** be at the ball on Saturday night.

2. When expressing intent or promise in the second and third persons.

> The police **shall** make the perpetrators responsible for their actions.
>
> We **shall** overcome the considerable obstacles against our company's financial future.

SENTENCE CONSTRUCTION

➤ *Should* vs. *would*

Would is used in all circumstances except in instances that express a possibility, a probability, or an obligation/requirement of some kind. In those cases, *should* is used.

> **Should he call** this afternoon, tell him the meeting has been cancelled. (*Possibility.*)
>
> I **should get** that completed form to you by next Tuesday. (*Probability.*)
>
> Bill **should stay** late this afternoon to make up for his long lunch hour. (*Requirement/obligation.*)

💣 **Caution:** Do not use *shall* and *should* interchangeably.

Perfect tenses

The perfect tenses indicate that an action was or will be completed before another time or action. The perfect tenses consist of the verb's past participle preceded by a form of the helping verb *have*.

✔ **Present perfect**

➤ An action that was done in the past, but continues into the present.

➤ Form the present perfect by using *has* or *have* (singular or plural as determined by the subject) and a past form of the main verb.

> As of today, Mary **has finished** only four of the six documents.
>
> The feud between Operations and Marketing **has gone** on for years.

✔ **Past perfect**

➤ An action that was finished before a second action, both in the past.

➤ Form the past perfect by using *had* with a past form of the main verb.

> I **had sent** the report before I received your request.
>
> Linda **had already left** the office by the time he called.

✔ **Future perfect**

➤ An action that will be finished by some specific time in the future, or before some other future event occurs.

➤ Form the future perfect by combining *will have* with a past form of the main verb.

> By the time I see you, I **will have finished** my master's degree.
>
> Peter **will have spoken** to Linda before the meeting on Thursday.

SENTENCE CONSTRUCTION

Verb tense and usage

Verb tense	Is used for	Example
Simple present	Actions taking place in the present	write
Present perfect	A finished action that is part of a continuing series of actions	has written, have written
Simple past	A finished past action	wrote
Past perfect	A finished past action that preceded another finished past action	had written
Simple future	A future action	will write
Future perfect	A future action that will be completed before another future action, or by a specific future time	will have written

Subjunctive voice

The subjunctive voice is used to express something that is not presently true: a wish, a suggestion, or a condition that is contrary to fact.

➤ Use either the past tense or *were* in the part of the sentence that is not true (often, the part of the sentence with the word *if*).

> I wish I **were** not so run-down with the flu.
>
> If Nick **insulted** people less often, he would have a better relationship with his coworkers.

💣 **Caution:** Do not use *would have* in place of *had* in an if clause.

Incorrect:
> If Nick **would have** insulted people less often at work, he might still have a job.

Correct:
> If Nick **had** insulted people less often at work, he might still have a job.

➤ After verbs that express desire (demand, insist, require, recommend) use the infinitive form of the verb without the *to*.

> I demand that you **return** the receipts, or you will not be reimbursed.
>
> The school recommends that you **submit** three letters of recommendation.

SENTENCE CONSTRUCTION

Modifiers

The simplest way to expand sentences is to add modifiers to describe or limit the nouns and verbs. Modifying words add detail.

✔ **Adjectives**

➤ Nouns are subjects or objects, and they are described by adjectives. Adjectives can "decorate" a noun and provide significantly more information about it.

➤ Adjectives usually precede the noun unless they are being used as predicate adjectives (completers) and follow the verb.

➤ Adjectives generally describe size, shape, color, emotion, condition, position, physical attribute, or some other quality.

➤ The words *a*, *an*, *and* the are considered adjectives (they are usually called "articles") and always precede a noun or noun phrase.

➤ Adjectives give color and vibrance to our language by allowing us to create word pictures for our readers. We can recreate the world around us in our writing.

➤ As a general rule, if you are using a series of adjectives, you should place size or shape first; color second; position, condition, or emotion next; and other qualities last.

> **Provides limited information:**
>   secretary
>
> **Provides more information:**
>   experienced secretary
>   stressed-out secretary
>   young secretary
>   angry secretary
>   nervous secretary
>
> **Provides even more information:**
>   nervous young secretary

&⌒**See also**: Absolute adjectives, *Common Sentence Problems* section

✔ **Adverbs**

➤ Adverbs do all of the other descriptive jobs in a sentence.

➤ Adverbs describe **verbs**:

> She thinks **quickly**.
> The new copy machine arrived **promptly**.

➤ Adverbs describe other **adverbs**:

> She thinks **very** quickly.
> The new copy machine arrived **rather** promptly.

SENTENCE CONSTRUCTION

➤ Adverbs describe **adjectives**:

> It was a **very** long letter.
> It was a **quite** negative report.

➤ Most adverbs are created by adding *–ly* to an adjective:

> sweet   ⟶   sweetly
> scarce   ⟶   scarcely
> prompt   ⟶   promptly
> rapid   ⟶   rapidly
> careful   ⟶   carefully

➤ Other adverbs state **how, when, where,** or **why**:

afterward	sometimes	so
beforehand	again	almost
generously	briefly	close
never	hard	helpfully
rather	sadly	now
satisfactorily	seldom	temporarily
soon	there	then
always	far	too
fast	rarely	very
here	since	well

✔ **Adjective vs. adverb**

Writers sometimes incorrectly use an adjective where they should use an adverb. Following are some common mistakes:

Incorrect:
> Call us direct to receive your subscription.

Correct:
> Call us **directly** to receive your subscription.

Incorrect:
> The manager was real pleased with the result.

Correct:
> The manager was **really** pleased with the result.

Incorrect:
> She sure did a good job!

Correct:
> She **surely** did a good job!

💣 **Caution:** Bad/badly. *Bad* should be used only as an adjective; the adverb is *badly.*

> He felt **bad** because his tooth ached **badly**.

↩ **See also**: Modifier problems, *Common Sentence Problems* section

SENTENCE BRIDGES

To complete your understanding of how sentences are put together, consider the ways ideas are linked. Two kinds of "sentence bridges" exist: prepositions and conjunctions.

Prepositions

✔ A preposition is a small bridge. It links only a noun or pronoun to the remainder of the sentence.

> John walked **into** the office.
>
> Susan put the report **on** the table.
>
> We must finish this project **by** Friday.

✔ A preposition, its object, and any words in between form a prepositional phrase. You can find prepositional phrases anywhere in sentences. Neither the subject nor the verb can ever be part of a prepositional phrase.

> **(In the meantime,)** we will process your request.
>
> The letters and memos **(on the desk)** are waiting **(for revision.)**

☞ **See also**: Dangling prepositions, *Common Sentence Problems* section

Common Prepositions

about	beneath	in spite of	since
above	beside	instead of	through
according to	between	into	throughout
across	beyond	like	till
after	by	near	to
against	concerning	next to	toward
along	despite	of	under
along with	down	off	underneath
among	during	on	unlike
around	except	onto	until
as	except for	out	up
aside from	excepting	out of	upon
at	for	outside	with
because of	from	over	within
before	in	past	without
behind	in addition to	regarding	
below	inside	round	

Conjunctions

✔ A conjunction is a bridge that links words, phrases, or clauses.

> Win **or** lose.
>
> John wrote the report, **but** Mary typed it.

TYPES OF SENTENCES

There are several types of sentences, and with the flexibility to combine various kinds of clauses, you can create any sentence you desire.

Independent clauses

✔ Independent clauses are simply complete thoughts with subjects and verbs. When capitalized and finished with a period, question mark, or exclamation point, an independent clause is also a complete sentence.

> The sky darkened.
>
> The school teaches students.

💣 **Caution:** Include a verb to avoid a sentence fragment.

> *Sentence fragment:*
> The baboon in the cage.

Dependent clauses

✔ Dependent clauses are groups of words with a subject and verb that do not express a complete thought.

> **Because the school teaches parents,** it is unusual.
>
> Parents **who are illiterate** often avoid their children's schools.

TYPES OF SENTENCES

Compound sentences

✔ A compound sentence consists of two independent clauses joined by a (coordinating) conjunction.

> Last July was hot, but August was even hotter.
>
> The hot sun scorched the land to powder, and the lack of rain made the soil untillable.

💣 **Caution:** Be sure to use a conjunction to prevent a comma splice.

> *Comma splice:*
> Last July was hot, August was even hotter.

Complex sentences

✔ A complex sentence consists of at least one independent clause and at least one dependent clause.

> Rain finally came, although many had left the area by then. *(Main clause, then dependent clause.)*
>
> When the rain came, people rejoiced. *(Dependent clause, then main clause.)*

COMMON SENTENCE PROBLEMS

Sentence fragments

✔ A dependent clause standing alone, trying to act as an independent idea, is not a complete sentence. The sentence does not contain a complete thought. Simply finishing the thought will correct the problem.

> *Example:*
> Because it was raining.

> *Better:*

We left early because it was raining.

🖋 **Note:** If you reverse the sentence order so that the dependent clause comes first, always place a comma after the dependent clause.

Because it was raining, we left early.

Run-on sentences

✔ This kind of sentence is longer than usual, contains several connected ideas, and lacks correct punctuation.

> *Example:*
> John finished his report early before he left for the meeting but since he still had four additional memos to complete he returned to his office after the meeting and worked until midnight writing project status reports.

> *Better:*

John finished his report early before he left for the meeting. Since he still had four additional memos to complete, he returned to his office after the meeting and worked until midnight writing project status reports.

🖋 **Note:** The average sentence today has approximately 16 to 18 words. You can write a sentence of up to 20 words with no loss of comprehension by your reader. If a sentence goes beyond 20 words, however, many readers may have difficulty understanding it.

COMMON SENTENCE PROBLEMS

Modifier problems

A modifier is a word or group of words that describes a noun or pronoun. It must appear near that noun or pronoun. Two types of modifier problems are seen in sentences: dangling modifiers and misplaced modifiers.

✔ **Dangling modifiers**
If the noun or pronoun being described (or modified) is not specifically named, the result can be confusing or silly.

Incorrect:
Walking through the office, the computer was turned on.

Correct:

Walking through the office, Mary stopped to turn on the computer.

Incorrect:
Checking the payment stubs, several errors were spotted.

Correct:

Checking the payment stubs, the clerk spotted several errors.

✔ **Misplaced modifiers**
If the modifier is not located near the noun or pronoun it is describing, the meaning may be ridiculous, vague, or confusing.

Incorrect:
When inflated with air, four people can be carried on this raft.

Correct:

When inflated with air, this raft can carry four people.

Incorrect:
She was employed for two years while going to school as a salesperson.

Correct:

While going to school, she was employed for two years as a salesperson.

See also: Modifiers, ***Sentence Construction*** section

COMMON SENTENCE PROBLEMS

Active vs. passive voice

Verbs are at the heart of sentences and can express active, powerful thoughts. The passive voice weakens verbs.

Voice means relationship. The two most powerful sentence elements, the subject and the verb, have a specific relationship. When the subject is the performer or "doer" of the verb, that active relationship is in the "active voice." If the subject is not the performer or "doer" of the verb, but instead is acted on by some other "doer," that passive relationship is in the "passive voice."

✔ Active voice tends to be:
- clearer/simpler
- more specific
- shorter
- easier to understand

Active:

> **The supervisor prepared** the new appraisal form.
>
> **Mary Grimes suggested** that the company change the sick leave policy.

✔ Passive voice tends to be:
- vague
- confusing
- longer
- dull, awkward

Passive:

> The new appraisal form **was prepared by the supervisor**.
>
> The sick leave policy **should be changed by the company** according to Mary Grimes' suggestion.

Sentence Parallelism

Sentences without good parallelism may be technically grammatically correct, but lack style, polish and clarity. Parallel sentences use the same parts of speech consistently:

Incorrect:
> The starlet demanded Golden Mountain spring water, eating freshly-picked fruit, and a Swedish massage every day.

Correct:
> The starlet demanded chilled spring water, fresh fruit and her own masseuse.

COMMON SENTENCE PROBLEMS

Dangling prepositions

It is common to ask, "Who are you going to lunch with?" or "Who should the report go to?"

While this is acceptable in casual, informal, "slangy" conversation, writing requires a higher standard. In writing, place the noun or pronoun at the end of the sentence.

> "Who is going to lunch with you?"
>
> "Who should receive copies of this report?"

✏ **Note:** Try to avoid placing a preposition at the end of a sentence.

👓 **See also:** Prepositions, *Sentence Bridges* section

Double negatives

✔ Using two negatives—known as a double negative—is generally considered incorrect as it conveys a meaning opposite of what the writer likely intended.

Incorrect:
> They **don't** know **nothing**.
> She **didn't** say **nothing** about the customer complaint.

Correct:
> They **don't** know **anything**.
> She **didn't** say **anything** about the customer complaint.

Double negatives are not always inappropriate. They may occasionally be deliberately employed to express a positive or to denote sarcasm or irony.

> When the off-duty paramedic saw the accident, he could **not** just sit and do **nothing** to help.
>
> I was **not** entirely **unhappy** to see him go.

COMMON SENTENCE PROBLEMS

Incorrect reflexives

✔ Memo writers frequently use the reflexive pronoun *-self* incorrectly as a subject or a verb. A reflexive pronoun cannot serve as a subject or object. It must "reflect" back to another pronoun that has already been used in the sentence.

Incorrect:
John and myself will attend the conference.

Correct:

> John and I will attend the conference.

Incorrect:
Send a copy of the report to Mary and myself.

Correct:

> Send a copy of the report to Mary and me.

Incorrect:
Call Linda or myself if you have questions.

Correct:

> Call Linda or me if you have questions.

Absolute adjectives

✔ Some adjectives should never be compared because there cannot be a greater degree of that quality.

Use	Not
unique	most unique
empty	emptiest
straight	most straight
complete	most complete
perfect	most perfect

✔ For pairing ideas, use *either/or* or *neither/nor*.

Incorrect:
He wanted neither a day off or extra pay

Correct:

> He wanted **neither** a day off **nor** extra pay.

Incorrect:
They asked him if he wanted a day off or extra pay.

Correct:

> They asked him if he wanted **either** a day off **or** extra pay.

🖙 **See also**: Modifiers, *Sentence Construction* section

COMMON SENTENCE PROBLEMS

Correct paragraph structure

As you work on developing better and more accurate sentence structure, remember that sentences are part of a larger picture: a good paragraph.

✔ Correct paragraphs contain:

1. A topic sentence naming the main idea being discussed. (*Preview the idea.*)
2. Support material such as facts, details, specific examples, evidence, and opinions that back up the main idea. (*State the idea.*)
3. A summary sentence that concludes or finishes the main idea. (*Review the idea.*)

PREVIEW — STATE — REVIEW

SPELLING

You can improve your spelling instantly by acquiring three habits:
- *Carefully proofread your writing.*
- *Cultivate a healthy suspicion of your spellings.*
- *Compulsively check a dictionary whenever you doubt a spelling.*

Exceptions

✔ Some groups of words are generally spelled a certain way, but have specific exceptions.

> *Examples:*

> Only one word in English ends in *-sede*: **supersede**.
>
> Only three words end in *-ceed*: **exceed, proceed,** and **succeed**.
>
> All other words in English that have the sound "seed" are spelled *-cede*: **concede, precede, intercede, accede, recede,** and **secede**.

Patterns

✔ Words ending in *c* almost always take the letter *k* before a suffix to retain the hard sound of the *c*.

mimic	⟶	mimicked
picnic	⟶	picnicking
panic	⟶	panicky
traffic	⟶	trafficked

✔ Most words that have the "eyes" sound at the end are spelled *-ize*.

authorize	criticize	organize
emphasize	vandalize	recognize
realize	minimize	prize
specialize	synthesize	

✔ A few such words end in *-ise*.

exercise	advise	franchise
merchandise	surprise	advertise
supervise	improvise	

SPELLING

Only a few "eyes" words end in -yze.

paralyze	analyze	catalyze

Most words that end with the "able" sound are also spelled -able.

admirable	dependable	probable
receivable	valuable	

However, some end in -ible.

compatible	responsible
terrible	feasible

Words ending in -ent, -ence, -ant, or -ance have no clearly identifiable pattern and usually need to be checked in the dictionary.

existent	resistant	defendant
relevance	intelligence	

💣 **Caution:** Pronounce your words carefully to avoid a misspelling (e.g., recognize, not reconize).

Helpful rules

1. Doubling a final consonant for a one-syllable word.

   ➤ If a one-syllable word ends in a single consonant preceded by a single vowel (as in *swim*), double the final consonant before any suffix starting with a vowel, or before the suffix y.

swim	swimmer	*not* swimer
beg	beggar	*not* begar
star	starry	*not* stary

   📕 **Exception:** In a one-syllable word ending in a y, preceded by a single vowel, **do not double** the y before any suffix beginning with a vowel.

buy	buyer	*not* buyyer
toy	toying	*not* toyying
joy	joyous	*not* joyyous

SPELLING

> If a one-syllable word ends in a single consonant preceded by a single vowel (as in *flag*), **do not double** the final consonant before any suffix beginning with a consonant.

flag	flagship	*not* flaggship
star	stardom	*not* starrdom
ship	shipment	*not* shippment

2. Doubling a final consonant for a multisyllable word.

> If a word of more than one syllable ends in a single consonant preceded by a single vowel (as in *defer*) and the accent rests on the final syllable, **double** the final consonant before any suffix starting with a vowel.

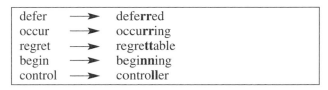

defer	⟶	deferred
occur	⟶	occurring
regret	⟶	regrettable
begin	⟶	beginning
control	⟶	controller

> If a word of more than one syllable ends in a single consonant preceded by a single vowel (as in *benefit*) and the accent does not fall on the last syllable, **do not double** the final consonant before any suffix starting with a vowel.

benefit	benefited	*not* benefitted
catalog	cataloged	*not* catalogged
borrow	borrowed	*not* borrowwed
credit	credited	*not* creditted
differ	differed	*not* differred
cancel	canceled	*not* cancelled
profit	profiting	*not* profitting

SPELLING

3. Words ending in *y*.

> ➤ If a word ends in *y* preceded by a consonant, change the *y* to *i* before adding any suffix except one beginning with *i*.

custody	⟶	custodial
ordinary	⟶	ordinarily
fancy	⟶	fanciful
defy	⟶	defiant
accompany	⟶	accompaniment
happy	⟶	happiness
academy	⟶	academic
economy	⟶	economist
but		
try	⟶	trying
lobby	⟶	lobbyist

> ➤ Words ending in *y* preceded by a vowel usually keep the *y* before any suffix.

display	⟶	displayed
employ	⟶	employable
buy	⟶	buyer
survey	⟶	surveyor
joy	⟶	joyful

Exceptions:

day	⟶	daily	*not* dayly
say	⟶	said	*not* sayed
pay	⟶	paid	*not* payed

Caution: Don't forget to add *-ly* to words ending in *l*.

accidental	⟶	accidentally
actual	⟶	actually
ideal	⟶	ideally

SPELLING

4. Words with *ei* and *ie*.

> Use the age-old rhyme, "Put *i* before *e*, except after *c*, or when sounded like *a*, as in 'neighbor' and 'weigh.' "

i before *e*:

belief	view
friend	anxiety
field	

Exceptions:

height	seize
foreign	either
forfeit	

Exceptions to "*e* before *i* after *c*":

deceive	receive	conceit	receipt

Exceptions to "*i* before *e* after *c*":

species	science	ancient

Exceptions to "sounded like *a*":

weight	deign	vein

5. Words ending in *e*.

> Words ending in a silent *e* usually drop the *e* before a suffix beginning with a vowel or a *y*.

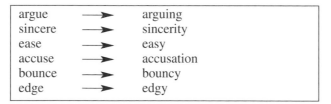

argue	⟶	arguing
sincere	⟶	sincerity
ease	⟶	easy
accuse	⟶	accusation
bounce	⟶	bouncy
edge	⟶	edgy

SPELLING

➤ Words ending in a silent *e* usually keep the *e* before a suffix beginning with a consonant.

hope	hopeful
nine	ninety
care	careless
like	likeness
manage	management
trouble	troublesome
flame	flameproof

6. Words ending in *ce* and *ge*.

➤ Words ending in *ce* or *ge* usually:

❖ Keep the *e* before a suffix beginning with *a* or *o*.

enforce	enforceable
courage	courageous
knowledge	knowledgeable
advantage	advantageous
peace	peaceable

❖ Drop the *e* before a suffix beginning with *i*.

finance	financial
enforce	enforcing
college	collegiate

🖊 **Note:** Every one of the spelling rules has exceptions.

SPELLING

General recommendations

1. Your computer's spell checker will pick up many common mistakes. There are, however, specific incorrect usages and look-alike or sound-alike words that spell checkers cannot identify. Therefore, you should not depend completely on a spell checker.

2. Create a list of your most typically misspelled words, and learn rules for consistent problems.

3. Read hard copy backward so that you don't get into the habit of skimming when you proofread.

4. Watch your pronunciation and say words correctly so that you hear all the appropriate sounds. Mispronunciation leads to misspelling.

5. Touch a word as you check it to help you focus on a single word at a time.

6. Be careful of words that have two acceptable spellings. The preferred spelling is always listed first in the dictionary. Become comfortable with your dictionary and thesaurus.

7. Pay special attention to long words—writers often leave out a letter or two in the middle.

8. Learn specific spelling rules such as the ones in this section.

9. Be careful of similar suffixes such as *er, ed, en*, and *es*. Fast typists may hit the wrong key, and a spell checker won't catch it.

10. Create a mental association with a difficult part of the word.

> *Examples:*
> attendance: attending a **dance**
> loneliness: feeling a**lone**

USAGE

Expressing yourself clearly and effectively depends greatly on the words you choose and how you use them in sentences. The English language offers a rich and extensive vocabulary, but it also harbors a wealth of look-alike, sound-alike words that can confuse your message.

accept/except

✔ **accept** (*verb*)
Receive willingly; agree to; consent to.

> John will **accept** the award at the luncheon on Thursday.

✔ **except** (*preposition*)
Other than; with the exclusion of.

> All of the reports **except** Linda's have been turned in.

adapt/adept/adopt

✔ **adapt** (*verb*)
To adjust to fit the needs.

> You can **adapt** the report template to suit the information you wish to convey.

✔ **adept** (*adjective*)
Proficient; extremely skilled.

> Angry customers soon calm down when Ellison speaks with them; she is **adept** at making people feel relaxed.

✔ **adopt** (*verb*)
To choose.

> If we **adopt** the new rules for our meetings, things will be more orderly.

adherence/adherents

✔ **adherence** (*noun*)
Attachment; following closely.

> Rules will only work if everyone is in **adherence** to them.

✔ **adherents** (*plural noun*)
Supporters; followers.

> The **adherents** of the new proposal made sure they were at the meeting in order to show their support.

USAGE

adverse/averse

✔ **adverse** (*adjective*)
Unfavorable, hostile.

> The President was opposed to **adverse** criticism.

✔ **averse** (*adjective*)
Opposed (usually used with "to").

> The President was **averse** to hostile criticism.

affect/effect

✔ **affect** (*verb*)
To influence (most common usage).

> The new policy will **affect** employee morale in a positive way.

✔ **affect** (*noun*)
Feeling or emotion (rare usage).

> The patient demonstrated little **affect** during the session.

✔ **effect** (*verb*)
To bring about, to cause (rare usage).

> The cost reduction program will **effect** layoffs of some staff members.

✔ **effect** (*noun*)
Result, outcome (most common usage).

> What **effect** will the equipment malfunction have on shipment of the orders?

aid/aide

✔ **aid** (*verb*)
To help.

> I would appreciate it if you could **aid** me in finding conference room 2B.

✔ **aide** (*noun*)
An assistant.

> The department will be hiring an **aide** to help with all the paperwork this project is generating.

USAGE

allude/elude

✔ **allude** (*verb*)
To make an indirect reference.

> At the staff meeting, the manager **alluded** to the customer service complaints.

✔ **elude** (*verb*)
To escape detection.

> The errors in the report **eluded** the proofreader.

allusion/illusion

✔ **allusion** (*noun*)
Indirect reference.

> Harriet made an **allusion** to the other company's profitability in her status report.

✔ **illusion** (*noun*)
An erroneous, false perception.

> Perfect morale is an **illusion** in many companies today.

alternate/alternative

✔ **alternate** (*noun*)
In place of another; substitute.

> I was selected as an **alternate**, to be there in case one of the jurors cannot finish the whole trial.

✔ **alternative** (*adjective*)
One of several things from which to choose.

> Though several **alternatives** to the current method exist, the team only tried one before scrapping the project altogether.

USAGE

among/between

✔ **among** (*preposition*)
Used to describe relationships involving more than two people or things.

> The four of them decided **among** themselves where they wanted to have dinner.

✔ **between** (*preposition*)
Used to describe relationships involving only two or for comparing one thing to a group to which it belongs.

> The choice was **between** New York and Los Angeles.

ante-/anti-

✔ **ante-** (*prefix*)
Prefix meaning "before."

> We dedicate this memorial to our ancestors, to our **ante**cedents in the community, to all those who have come before us.

✔ **anti-** (*prefix*)
Prefix meaning "against."

> I hope my **anti**perspirant lasts through the meeting; I don't want them to see me break a sweat.

anxious/eager

✔ **anxious** (*adjective*)
Worried; disturbed; concerned.

> The **anxious** secretary checked three times for the overnight delivery.

✔ **eager** (*adjective*)
Enthusiastic; interested; keen.

> Susan was **eager** to start her new job.

USAGE

appraise/apprise

✔ **appraise** (*verb*)
To evaluate; to judge; to estimate.

> The head of Risk Management will **appraise** the four buildings before issuing insurance policies.

✔ **apprise** (*verb*)
To inform; to tell; to notify.

> I will **apprise** you of the board's decision immediately after Tuesday's meeting.

bases/basis

✔ **bases** (*plural noun*)
Plural of "base" and of "basis."

> Let's make sure we cover all the **bases** of our pitch again before we make our final presentation.

✔ **basis** (*noun*)
A foundation upon which something rests.

> On the **basis** of your stunning letters of recommendation, we have decided to hire you for the position.

bizarre/bazaar

✔ **bizarre** (*adjective*)
Strikingly unconventional; odd; weird.

> I knew something **bizarre** was happening when the elevator was filled with balloons.

✔ **bazaar** (*noun*)
A market.

> Every week during the summer a **bazaar** sets up in the parking lot to sell crafts and snacks.

USAGE

broach/brooch

✔ **broach** (*verb*)
To introduce.

> I hate to **broach** the subject, but have you found out what led to Alan quitting last week?

✔ **brooch** (*noun*)
A piece of jewelry.

> I don't usually wear jewelry, but my grandmother gave me this **brooch** recently and she's meeting me for lunch.

capital/capitol

✔ **capital** (*noun*)
Assets; money; seat of state government; uppercase letter.

> The new plant represents a major **capital** investment.
> Denver is the **capital** of Colorado.
> Start each sentence with a **capital** letter.

✔ **capitol** (*noun*)
Building where the legislature meets.

> **Capitol** Hill is usually a frenzy of activity.

cash/cache

✔ **cash** (*noun*)
Money (slang).

> We have the **cash** to invest now, and we need to act while the market is hot.

✔ **cache** (*noun*)
A hiding place.

> I know there is a **cache** of chocolate around here somewhere, just in case of emergencies.

USAGE

casual/causal

✔ **casual** (*adjective*)
Incidental; not formal.

> We had a **casual** discussion about the case when we passed in the hall, but we did not have any meetings about it yet.

✔ **causal** (*adjective*)
Expresses cause; relates to or constitutes a cause.

> The **causal** factor in the company's debt is that it spent more money than it took in.

chord/cord

✔ **chord** (*noun*)
A combination of musical notes.

> The opening **chord** of this piece of music is a perfect representation of the energy our product delivers. Let's use it in the commercial.

✔ **cord** (*noun*)
String or rope.

> Tie up this bundle of catalogues with **cord** so we can recycle them.

cite/sight/site

✔ **cite** (*verb*)
To quote an authority; to acknowledge.

> Linda **cited** the first three quarterly reports in her year-end summary.

✔ **sight** (*noun*)
Ability to see.

> Bill did not lose **sight** of problems in Operations when he moved to Purchasing.

✔ **site** (*noun*)
Location or place.

> Our company has three remote **sites** where manufacturing takes place.

USAGE

climatic/climactic

✔ **climatic** (*adjective*)
Relating to climate.

> There will be some **climatic** discomfort in the office until the air conditioning is repaired.

✔ **climactic** (*adjective*)
Relating to climax; the highest point.

> Of course, the most **climactic** point of the conference occurred when the whiteboard fell over onto the laser projector and burst into flames.

complement/compliment

✔ **complement** (*verb*)
To complete or add value to something.

> The new safety program will **complement** perfectly the OSHA regulations implemented January 1.

✔ **complement** (*noun*)
Something that completes or brings to perfection.

> The wine was a delicious **complement** to the meal.

✔ **compliment** (*verb*)
To praise.

> Susan **complimented** the staff on a job well done.

✔ **compliment** (*noun*)
An expression of praise.

> Bill was embarrassed by the **compliment**.

USAGE

conscience/conscious

✔ **conscience** (*noun*)
A sense of right and wrong.

> Only someone with a complete lack of **conscience** would bilk old ladies out of their savings.

✔ **conscious** (*adjective*)
Fully aware.

> I am **conscious** of the fact that sometimes you need to spend money to make money, but there are limits.

continual/continuous

✔ **continual** (*adjective*)
Occurring steadily, but with occasional stops or breaks.

> Because he **continually** missed his deadlines, he received a verbal warning.

✔ **continuous** (*adjective*)
Unbroken, occurring without pauses, stops, or breaks.

> Niagara Falls receives a **continuous** flow of water from the river.

council/counsel/consul

✔ **council** (*noun*)
An advisory or legislative body.

> Sandra's position on the Executive **Council** will last for two years.

✔ **counsel** (*noun*)
Advice or help.

> Mary sought **counsel** from Brian about whether or not she should interview for the new position.

✔ **counsel** (*verb*)
To advise.

> The dietitian will **counsel** the patient about nutritious meal plans.

✔ **consul** (*noun*)
A government official who resides in a foreign city and represents fellow citizens there.

> The **consul** promised to check into the snarled paperwork.

USAGE

criticize/critique

✔ **criticize** (*verb*)
To judge negatively.

> It is a bad idea to **criticize** our new programs in front of the fund raisers who made them possible in the first place.

✔ **critique** (*verb*)
To evaluate.

> Now that the project is complete, I'd like to **critique** our process so we know what to repeat, and what aspects need changing.

decent/descent/dissent

✔ **decent** (*adjective*)
Proper, adequate, passable.

> If we do a **decent** job at promoting this product, it will fly off the shelves.

✔ **descent** (*noun*)
The act of moving downward.

> The **descent** of the company to second in the market is unacceptable to the driven CEO.

✔ **dissent** (*noun*)
Disagreement.

> The **dissent** in the room was audible in the loud groans we heard when the idea was presented.

deduce/deduct

✔ **deduce** (*verb*)
To infer, to draw a conclusion.

> I **deduce** from your wet umbrella that it is still raining outside.

✔ **deduct** (*verb*)
To subtract from.

> My balance is low because every week I **deduct** more from my account than I put in.

USAGE

defuse/diffuse

✔ **defuse** (*verb*)
To make less harmful, potent, or tense.

> A trained negotiator can **defuse** a difficult situation between irritated parties.

✔ **diffuse** (*verb*)
To spread out; to scatter.

> The lamps in the waiting room are too harsh; we need shades to **diffuse** the light.

disapprove/disprove

✔ **disapprove** (*verb*)
To express lack of approval.

> I **disapprove** of the way that some people take two-hour lunches and leave the work to the rest of us.

✔ **disprove** (*verb*)
To prove false.

> The fact that our department is first in sales this quarter should **disprove** all those who criticized our plan.

disburse/disperse

✔ **disburse** (*verb*)
To pay out.

> The comptroller will not **disburse** the funds until the proper signatures have been received.

✔ **disperse** (*verb*)
To scatter.

> The police asked the crowd to **disperse** after the party got out of hand.

USAGE

disinterested/uninterested

✔ **disinterested** (*adjective*)
Impartial, fair, and objective.

> Sally was asked to be a **disinterested** member of the committee in formulating the new policy.

✔ **uninterested** (*adjective*)
Not interested.

> Tom is **uninterested** in participating in the flex-time program.

elicit/illicit

✔ **elicit** (*verb*)
To draw forth.

> I tried to **elicit** a response from Jasper about what to order for lunch, but he said nothing.

✔ **illicit** (*adjective*)
Amoral.

> The **illicit** ivory trade has led to the poaching of animals for nothing but their tusks.

elusive/illusive

✔ **elusive** (*adjective*)
Hard to catch.

> The goal is **elusive** for now, but once we have a decent team together, success will be ours.

✔ **illusive** (*adjective*)
Unreal; imaginary.

> The **illusive** Phoenix is an appropriate symbol for rebirth and renewal.

USAGE

emerge/immerge

✔ **emerge** (*verb*)
To rise out of.

> Green shoots began to **emerge** from the soil soon after the bulbs were planted.

✔ **immerge** (*verb*)
To plunge into.

> **Immerge** your hand in cold water immediately so it won't swell.

eminent/immanent/imminent

✔ **eminent** (*adjective*)
Well-known.

> We are fortunate to have an **eminent** scholar on Egyptian sculpture as our lecturer today.

✔ **immanent** (*adjective*)
Existing within; inherent.

> Some feel that greed is **immanent** in human nature, while others believe in honest human kindness.

✔ **imminent** (*adjective*)
Impending; soon to arrive.

> Alesander spent all his time on the phone making arrangements for his imminent vacation.

everyday/every day

✔ **everyday** (*adjective*)
Ordinary.

> We should use the special china for dinner tonight; receiving a promotion is not an **everyday** occurrence!

✔ **every day** (*adjective*) (*noun*)
Each day.

> Make sure to back up your data **every day** before you leave the office.

USAGE

exalt/exult

✔ **exalt** (*verb*)
To raise in rank; glorify.

> Allison was **exalted** and given another promotion for doubling the client base upon taking over the department.

✔ **exult** (*verb*)
To rejoice.

> While we all want to **exult** in the moment of our team's victory, destruction of property is no way to show one's joy.

farther/further

✔ **farther** (*adverb*)
Additional to actual distance.

> The office that you are looking for is just a little **farther** down the hall.

✔ **further** (*adjective*)
To a greater extent.

> We will have to **further** discuss the new line at the next departmental meeting.

formally/formerly

✔ **formally** (*adverb*)
In compliance with rules, procedures, regulations.

> She soon will be **formally** installed as president of the Management Club.

✔ **formerly** (*adverb*)
In the past; some time ago.

> He was **formerly** in charge of Accounting and now runs Purchasing.

USAGE

fourth/forth

✔ **fourth** (*adjective*)
Preceded by three others in a series.

> Ellen is the **fourth** secretary we've had in Human Resources.

✔ **forth** (*adverb*)
Forward; onward.

> The manager gave us permission to go **forth** with the project.

healthful/healthy

✔ **healthful** (*adjective*)
Promotes good health.

> Eating three **healthful** meals a day can prevent many illnesses.

✔ **healthy** (*adjective*)
In good health.

> People need to eat properly in order to remain **healthy**.

imply/infer

✔ **imply** (*verb*)
To suggest.

> I hope you don't mean to **imply** that I have done something to sabotage your project.

✔ **infer** (*verb*)
To guess or conclude.

> One might **infer**, from the anger you are showing, that this news is quite upsetting to you.

USAGE

indict/indite

✔ **indict** (*verb*)
To charge with a crime.

> The committee can make investigations into the wrong-doing, but only a judge can **indict** the perpetrators.

✔ **indite** (*verb*)
To write.

> It will take me just a minute to **indite** my greetings on the birthday card.

inequity/iniquity

✔ **inequity** (*noun*)
Unfairness.

> I am incredibly concerned about the **inequity** of the division of labor between my coworker and me, because I seem to do much more than he.

✔ **iniquity** (*noun*)
A wicked act or thing.

> The **iniquity** of emptying out the pensions of elderly retirees to make the company appear more profitable should be punished to the highest degree.

ingenious/ingenuous

✔ **ingenious** (*adjective*)
Clever.

> Magda has come up with an **ingenious** solution to the problem that will save an incredible amount of time.

✔ **ingenuous** (*adjective*)
Naïve; openly straightforward.

> Evan's **ingenuous** description of the problems in this department should not be misconstrued as slander; he really wants to make things better around here.

USAGE

lay/lie

✔ **lay** (*verb*)
To place.

> Please **lay** the report on the table so Alice will see it when she comes in.

✔ **lie** (*verb*)
To recline.

> After struggling for ten hours with getting all the boxes into the house, I will **lie** down for an hour.

learn/teach

✔ **learn** (*verb*)
To receive knowledge from something or someone.

> Penny **learned** the new computer program quickly.

✔ **teach** (*verb*)
To impart knowledge to someone else.

> Each of the supervisors will **teach** New Employee Orientation.

let/leave

✔ **let** (*verb*)
To allow or permit something.

> Ellen **let** me borrow her copy of the annual report.

✔ **leave** (*verb*)
To go away; to depart.

> Sally must **leave** for the meeting immediately after lunch.

USAGE

liable/libel

✔ **liable** (*adjective*)
Legally obligated; responsible.

> We are **liable** for any injury that happens on our property.

✔ **libel** (*noun*)
Defamatory statement.

> **Libel** against our company is not tolerated; our attorneys send letters to those who slander our good name.

loath/loathe

✔ **loath** (*adjective*)
Unwilling or reluctant.

> I am **loath** to start the inventory of the back warehouse, because it is a messy job.

✔ **loathe** (*verb*)
To hate.

> I **loathe** days like this when I miss my train, spill my coffee, and delete important files all before noon.

lose/loose

✔ **lose** (*verb*)
To be unable to find or obtain.

> Jenny was afraid she would **lose** the bid.

✔ **loose** (*verb*)
To make free; untie.

> Why **loose** your anger on me?

USAGE

maybe/may be

✔ **maybe** (*adverb*)
Perhaps.

> **Maybe** we can ask the Quality Team to address the Customer Service issues.

✔ **may be** (*verb*)
A possibility exists.

> It **may be** that the meeting will be delayed, because Ms. Jensen has not yet returned to the office.

moral/morale

✔ **moral** (*adjective*)
Virtuous.

> The way to determine the **moral** thing to do in a situation is to think of how you would like to be treated.

✔ **morale** (*noun*)
Spirit.

> The best way to keep up company **morale** is to acknowledge when someone has done a good job.

persecute/prosecute

✔ **persecute** (*verb*)
To oppress.

> Throughout history, it seems that one group is always **persecuting** another through wars and invasions.

✔ **prosecute** (*verb*)
To sue.

> We are going to **prosecute** this case against those who embezzled from the pension fund and, hopefully, reclaim some money for the retirees.

USAGE

personal/personnel

✔ **personal** (*adjective*)
Private; individual; involving one person.

> The manager asked her assistant to do several **personal** errands.

✔ **personnel** (*noun*)
Employees of an organization.

> Acme hired several new **personnel** to complete the conversion project.

✔ **personnel** (*adjective*)
Referring to employees.

> The **Personnel** Department is responsible for all hiring functions.

perspective/prospective

✔ **perspective** (*noun*)
A view.

> There is a better **perspective** of the stage from the balcony.

✔ **prospective** (*adjective*)
Likely or expected to happen.

> The **prospective** hires had to complete a personality inventory and present a five-minute report about some area of business.

plaintiff/plaintive

✔ **plaintiff** (*noun*)
Party suing in a lawsuit.

> The **plaintiff** alleges that the defendant willfully neglected his legal duties.

✔ **plaintive** (*adjective*)
Mournful.

> The grieving man let out a **plaintive** cry.

USAGE

populace/populous

✔ **populace** (*noun*)
The masses; the general public.

> The **populace** is now equipped with ever smaller media recording devices that only specialists had previously.

✔ **populous** (*adjective*)
Heavily settled.

> This area has become so **populous** over the past decade that the county is revisiting the zoning laws in hopes of keeping a check on the population growth.

precede/proceed

✔ **precede** (*verb*)
To go before.

> The groom and the attendants should all **precede** the bride down the aisle.

✔ **proceed** (*verb*)
To go forward.

> After the wedding, we will all **proceed** to the restaurant for the reception.

USAGE

principal/principle

✔ **principal** (*adjective*)
First in rank or importance.

> The financial security was the **principal** reason he joined the firm.

✔ **principal** (*noun*)
The person in a lead position or the head of an educational institution; a sum of money that earns interest.

> The **principal** called an all-school assembly to announce the awards.

> The **principal** plus interest is due in 45 days.

✔ **principle** (*noun*)
A fundamental truth or law.

> Ben practices the **principles** of ethical management.

rebut/refute

✔ **rebut** (*verb*)
To argue in opposition.

> Marisol **rebutted** the opposition's argument that the workplace was safe with the documented conditions that existed in the factory at that time.

✔ **refute** (*verb*)
To prove wrong.

> The photos and workers' statements were more than enough to **refute** the opposition's argument of workplace safety.

USAGE

regardless/irrespective/irregardless

✔ **regardless** (*adverb*)
Without regard for objections; anyway.

> **Regardless** of his feelings, she took the new job.

✔ **irrespective** (*adverb*)
Without consideration of; regardless of.

> The departmental bonus is disbursed among everyone equally, **irrespective** of individual merit.

✔ **irregardless**
Not a real word. Some writers mistakenly use *irregardless* to mean "without regard," but the prefix *ir* is unnecessary, since *regardless* is already negative.

respectively/respectfully

✔ **respectively** (*adverb*)
In a proper sequence or order.

> Chris was elected to the positions of vice president and treasurer, **respectively**.

✔ **respectfully** (*adverb*)
With respect.

> The new director spoke **respectfully** of his predecessor.

simple/simplistic

✔ **simple** (*adjective*)
Clear and easy to understand.

> The directions are **simple**: add hot water and drink.

✔ **simplistic** (*adjective*)
Oversimplified.

> "What goes up must come down" is a **simplistic** explanation for the destruction I see before me.

USAGE

stationery/stationary

✔ **stationery** (*noun*)
Writing paper and envelopes.

> We need to order new **stationery** for the office.

✔ **stationary** (*adjective*)
In a fixed position.

> Riding a **stationary** bicycle is a good form of exercise.

that/which

✔ **that** (*pronoun*)
Pronoun that refers to a part of the sentence integral to meaning.

> We are going to the building **that** is on the corner of First and Howard.

✔ **which** (*pronoun*)
A relative pronoun that designates additional detail or information.

> Room 24, **which** is down the hall, is where the conference is going to be held.

then/than

✔ **then** (*adverb*)
At a certain time, later.

> First, we'll send out the customer survey; **then** we'll develop the new program.

✔ **than** (*conjunction*)
A word used to introduce a comparison.

> Beth is better **than** Ellen at using the computer.

USAGE

two/too/to

✔ **two** (*adjective*)
The number 2.

> I need **two** copies of the Henderson report immediately.

✔ **too** (*adverb*)
In addition; more than; also; very.

> Our budget is **too** high at present.

✔ **to** (*preposition*)
Toward.

> Mary went **to** the meeting.

uninterested/disinterested

✔ **uninterested** (*adjective*)
Bored.

> She appeared totally **uninterested** in the conversation as she gazed out the window.

✔ **disinterested** (*adjective*)
Unbiased; objective.

> We need to bring in a **disinterested** third party to resolve this dispute.

veracious/voracious

✔ **veracious** (*adjective*)
Honest; truthful.

> Andy gave a **veracious** account of what had happened, despite the fact that people had encouraged him to lie.

✔ **voracious** (*adjective*)
Having a huge appetite; greedy.

> Elle is a **voracious** reader; her apartment is crammed with bookshelves.

USAGE

waive/wave

✔ **waive** (*verb*)
To give up (a claim or right).

> The contract stipulates that the author will produce the book as a work for hire and **waive** all future claims on royalties.

✔ **wave** (*verb*)
To gesture, to signal.

> With a **wave** of his hand, David signaled Alec to come into the office .

weather/whether

✔ **weather** (*noun*)
The state of the atmosphere.

> The **weather** prediction for the weekend is great: plenty of sun with few clouds.

✔ **whether** (*conjunction*)
Used to introduce stated or implied alternative possibility or possibilities.

> I do not know **whether** the art supply store will be open at this hour.

PUNCTUATION

Punctuation marks serve to organize or clarify written language. The rules of punctuation vary with language, location, and time.

Periods   •

Periods are the most frequently used punctuation marks to help signify the end of a complete thought. Periods are necessary for a number of important tasks.

☙ **Rules:**

✔ Use a period at the end of a complete sentence that is a statement.

> Mehret is the Vice President of International Markets.
>
> I understand that you have a significant amount of experience in running database programs.

✔ Use a period after an indirect question.

> Errol asked where the monthly report was.
>
> Yolanda wondered what was for dinner.

✔ If the last word in the sentence ends in a period, do not follow it with another period. Commas, question marks, and other punctuation should be used as they would usually.

> This is my first trip to the U.S.
>
> On Magnus's first trip to the U.S., he met lifelong friends.
>
> When do you think Krystle will stop talking about her Ph.D.?

✔ Use a period for some abbreviations.

> The samples were collected Aug. 6, 1952.
>
> All the food, decorations, silverware, etc., that we need for the event should be charged to the entertainment budget.

💣 **Caution:** There is no reliable rule for abbreviations: Some get periods, some do not. Only a dictionary will tell you for sure which do, though the information may differ from dictionary to dictionary, as each relies on its own measurement of standard usage to decide which is the "authoritative" usage for its lexicon.

PUNCTUATION

Commas   ,

Commas are among the most frequently used punctuation marks to help manage the flow of thoughts in a sentence. Commas perform many critical functions:

✎ Rules:

✔ Use a comma in a compound sentence where a conjunction (*and, but, or, yet, so, for, nor*) separates the complete thoughts.

> We expected an especially heavy workload today, so we asked for three temporary employees.
>
> Susan investigated the complaint, and Bill wrote a thorough report.

✔ Use a comma where consecutive adjectives modify the same noun.

> We prepared a hard-hitting, effective ad campaign.
>
> He wrote a thorough, detailed report.

✔ Use a comma before the final *and* or *or* in a series of three or more.

> Jane ordered pens, pencils, and stationery.
>
> John bought cookies, muffins, and fruit for the staff meeting.

✔ Use a comma between the dependent clause (incomplete thought) and the independent clause (complete thought) in a complex sentence. This is most typically done when sentence order is inverted (the incomplete thought comes first).

> If you need my assistance, please notify me by Friday.
>
> *Or:*
> Please notify me by Friday if you need my assistance.

> Because we had received a complaint, the manager interviewed each of the employees at the counter.
>
> *Or:*
> The manager interviewed each of the employees at the counter because we had received a complaint.

PUNCTUATION

✔ Use a comma for any introductory idea, interruption, or afterthought.

Introductory idea:

> In the meantime, we will continue the current policy.
>
> On Friday, July 17, the Personnel Department will conduct interviews for the three positions.

Interruption:

> Ellen Henderson, rather than Mary Phipps, was named manager of the Seattle office.
>
> You will see, however, that the project will be finished on time.

Afterthought:

> It's not too late to change the deadline, is it?
>
> Send the report to Data Processing by Monday, if you can.

✔ Use two commas to set off any expression that explains a preceding word.

> John Pickering, vice president of Acme Computers, is attending the meeting.
>
> Offshore manufacturing, a typical production option today, is helping to create a global village.

✔ Use commas to set off a year written after both the month and the day (to show exactly which month and day you mean).

> The August 30, 2005, report details our recovery of delinquent funds.
>
> The meeting on Tuesday, March 14, 2006, is to discuss the four final job candidates.

💣 **Caution:** Do not use commas for just a month and year.

> The December 1992 report showed significant gains in our customer response.
>
> Peter Montgomery was hired in January 1988.

PUNCTUATION

✔ Use commas to set off the name of a state or country after a city because it identifies a particular city.

> We know she lives in either Kansas City, Kansas, or Kansas City, Missouri.

Do not use a comma to separate:

1. A subject and its verb.
2. A verb and the object immediately following.
3. The two parts of a compound subject, compound verb, or compound object connected by *and*, *or*, or *but*.
4. A reflexive pronoun from the rest of the sentence.
5. A short prepositional phrase at the beginning of a sentence from the rest of that sentence.

Semicolons   ;

Semicolons are markers that separate various kinds of clauses and phrases. Being able to correctly identify clauses and phrases within a sentence is helpful in using semicolons correctly.

✍ Rules:

✔ Use a semicolon instead of a conjunction to join two complete thoughts. The two independent clauses, when joined, create a compound sentence.

> We know that customer service is important to quality efforts; we are implementing new evaluation procedures to solicit customer feedback.
>
> The employees are very supportive of the new forms; they are turning in completed ones at the end of every week.

PUNCTUATION

✔ Use a semicolon to join two complete thoughts (independent clauses) when the second one begins with a conjunctive adverb or transitional word (such as: *accordingly, also, consequently, further, however, indeed, in fact, moreover, nevertheless, then, therefore, thus*). The most commonly used transitions are *however* and *therefore*. If the connecting word has more than one syllable, place a comma after the connection.

> The computer program was difficult to learn; nevertheless, Susan continued her training program until she was proficient.
>
> Please tell Mr. Henson the nature of the complaint; then he can refer it to the appropriate department manager.
>
> We need your information on the project; therefore, we will schedule the meeting when you are available.

✔ Use a semicolon instead of a comma when two complete thoughts joined by a coordinating conjunction have other commas in the sentence.

> We need to order pens, pencils, and markers; and the order must be placed before March 20.
>
> She needs more assistance to finish the project; but the clerks, administrative assistants, and secretaries are all unavailable.

✔ Use a semicolon before an expression (or its abbreviation) such as *for example* (e.g.), *that is* (i.e.), and *namely*, if it introduces a list or explanation. Always use a comma after these expressions.

> The manager had one basic belief; namely, the customer is always right.
>
> Many cities would be suitable for the national conference; for example, New Orleans, Atlanta, Los Angeles, or Seattle.

✔ Use a semicolon to separate a series of items with internal commas. The semicolon clearly shows the major separations between the items.

> The ad hoc committee elected its new officers: Melissa Kendall, president; Hector Garcia, president-elect; Sondra Norman, vice president; and Andrew Grebecki, treasurer.

💣 **Caution:** A semicolon is an essential punctuation mark, but one that should not be overused. If you string too many thoughts together, sentences will become complicated and confusing. Instead, use semicolons to organize components into the clearest, most well-structured sentences possible.

PUNCTUATION

Colons   :

A colon is used primarily as a separator, dividing major sentence elements. Its most specific and well-known function is to call attention to whatever follows.

✒ Rules:

✔ Use a colon to formally introduce a list or an idea with a word or phrase such as: *the following, as follows, these, this*. The word after the colon is capitalized when it's the beginning of a complete sentence (or when the material following the colon consists of two or more sentences); it is not capitalized when the list or idea is not a sentence.

> Prepare the title page as follows: Write the full title and originating department in the center of the page.
>
> The real problems in manufacturing are: high turnover, equipment repair costs, and expensive shipping requirements.

✔ Use a colon after the salutation of a business letter, and after the words *subject* or *attention*.

> Dear Mr. Garcia:
>
> Attention:

✔ In business writing, use a colon to introduce a quotation of one long sentence, or two or more sentences of any length.

> The CEO addressed the board as follows: "We are creating a new marketing strategy to position our best-selling product more competitively."

✔ Use colons for separation.

> ➤ **Titles**
> Separate a title from a subtitle.

> The Earth: A Green Planet

      👁 **See also**: Titles, *Titles and Capitalization* section

PUNCTUATION

➤ **Time**

Separate hours from minutes.

> 8:19 a.m.; 4:07 p.m.

➤ **Citations**

Separate chapter from verse in a biblical reference.

> John 2:14

➤ **Ratios**

> 2:1

💣 **Caution:** Avoid using a colon between a verb and complement, verb and object, or preposition and object.

Incorrect:

> Two entertaining movies directed by Steven Spielberg are: *ET* and *Jaws*.

Correct:

> Two entertaining movies directed by Steven Spielberg are *ET* and *Jaws*.

Quotation marks   " "

Quotation marks—either double (" ") or single (' ')—mainly enclose direct quotations from speech and from writing. Always use quotation marks in pairs, one at the beginning of a quotation and one at the end.

✍ **Rules:**

✔ The main purpose of quotation marks is to indicate that you are using someone else's exact words, whether spoken or written. Enclose all exact quotations.

> On the telephone you stated: "We will send the invoices no later than June 21."
>
> I asked John, "Do you like 'The Raven' by Edgar Allen Poe?"

PUNCTUATION

➤ Do not use quotation marks to paraphrase; this is called an "indirect quotation."

> On the telephone you stated that you will send the invoices no later than June 21.

➤ Use a colon to introduce a quotation that relates directly to the previous part of the sentence.

> The vice president's reply was immediate: "We will implement the new program in 10 days."

➤ Use a comma to introduce a quotation of one short sentence.

> She said, "I'll finish that right away."

✔ Ending punctuation for a closing quotation mark is as follows:

➤ Periods and commas go inside a closing quotation mark.

> He said, "We'll have to revise our procedure."
>
> "The fact is," she said deliberately, "we must move on this before the end of the month."

➤ Semicolons and colons go outside a closing quotation mark.

> The staff members were told, "There is an impending wage reduction"; they chose to stay and continue to work toward profitability.
>
> The CEO provided the managers with a partial list of the "causes of the profit reduction": high interviewing and selection expenses, significant training costs, and a manufacturing redesign.

➤ Question marks, exclamation points, and dashes can go **either inside** or **outside** quotation marks.

They are placed **inside** when they relate specifically to the quoted items.

> "Incredible!" was all Mary could reply.
>
> "We're trying to—" was all she could say before the phone went dead.

PUNCTUATION

They are placed **outside** the quotes when they relate to the entire sentence.

Did you read the article, "Secure Your Future"?

"Give me liberty or give me death"—Patrick Henry is famous for this proclamation.

✔ Quotation marks are placed around titles of articles in magazines or chapters in books, poems, short stories, dissertations, plays, and lectures. The names of magazines, newspapers, and books are *italicized*, underlined, or written in ALL CAPITAL LETTERS rather than enclosed in quotation marks.

✔ Use quotation marks around technical terms (in nontechnical material), slang phrases, colloquial expressions, made-up or "coined" phrases, and deliberate mistakes in spelling.

This program is "user-friendly."

Brett wanted to "nail down" the details on the Smith proposal.

💣 **Caution:** Don't use quotation marks in an attempt to justify or apologize for slang and trite expressions that are inappropriate to your writing.

Incorrect:

We should support the President in his "hour of need" rather than "wimp out" on him.

Correct:

We should give the President the support he needs rather than turn away like cowards.

✍ **See also**: Quotations, *Titles and Capitalization* section

PUNCTUATION

Parentheses ( )

Parenthetical expressions include explanations, facts, digressions, and examples that may be helpful or interesting but are not essential to meaning. They are emphasized least when enclosed in parentheses rather than set off with commas or dashes.

✍Rules:

✔ Parentheses enclose expressions that are explanatory or supplementary to the main thought of a sentence. They may be comments from the author, additions to the meaning, or anything that is incidental to the sentence.

> The committee reviewed the agenda items (see Appendix A).

➤ Many writers use dashes instead of parentheses to set the material off more sharply.

> The proposal—and it was their final offer—was too good to turn down.

✔ Parentheses enclose numbers or letters in lists of running text.

> Exercise aids in (a) increasing aerobic heart function, (b) maintaining your weight, and (c) reducing your stress.

💣 **Caution:** Do not use parentheses to enclose numbers or letters in a tabulated list.

> Exercise aids in the following:
> a. Increasing aerobic heart function.
> b. Maintaining your weight.
> c. Reducing your stress.

✔ Parentheses enclose clarifications of quantities in a formal document.

> The consultant's fee for this contract shall be one thousand dollars ($1,000).

PUNCTUATION

✔ Punctuating with parentheses: As a general rule, never punctuate or capitalize a parenthetical expression that is inside another sentence. Capitalize and punctuate when the parenthetical thought is a separate sentence.

> The committee reviewed the agenda items and voted on them (see Appendix A).
>
> The committee reviewed the agenda items (see Appendix A) and voted on them.
>
> The committee reviewed the agenda items and voted on them. (See Appendix A.)

Dashes —

Use a dash or dashes to indicate sudden changes in tone or thought and to set off some sentence elements.

✎ Rules:

✔ The most common use of dashes is to indicate a major break in the flow of a thought.

> Mr. Johnson knows—or at least thinks he does—what the solution to the problem should be.

✔ Dashes also can emphasize an explanatory phrase.

> Sally needs to send out the report—the third-quarter report—immediately.

✔ Use a dash after an expression such as *that is* or *namely* when it introduces a tabulated list.

> John discovered four ways to improve quality; namely—
> 1. reduce expenses
> 2. listen to the customers
> 3. improve design
> 4. limit inventory

PUNCTUATION

✔ Use a dash before any word or phrase that sums up a series ahead of it.

> Quality, responsiveness, attention—these are the
> promises we make to our customers.
>
> Susan Adams, Bill Eversol, Beth Winston—any of these
> employees could serve on the United Way campaign.

💣 **Caution:** Although dashes also can take the place of commas, semicolons, or parentheses, remember: Overuse of the dash weakens its dramatic effect on the reader. Used sparingly, it highlights, sharpens, and strengthens your message. Overused, dashes make your writing choppy and difficult to read. A proficient business writer uses the dash only to achieve a special emphasis.

✎ **Note:** Create a dash by striking the hyphen key twice, with no space in front, between, or behind the hyphens. Although written material can be found with a space preceding and following the dash, the most common use of the dash is written without spaces.

Hyphens   -

A hyphen is used primarily for word division or to join words to create a new word.

✎**Rules:**

✔ The hyphen divides a word that cannot be completed at the end of a line.

> Admirers credited Ty's meteoric rise to hard work and
> dedication, but insiders knew it was also due to his mega-
> lomaniacal ambition.

✔ Hyphenate compound words that start with *self, anti, ex, pro, post, mid,* etc.

self-defeating	self-evident
self-centered	self-esteem
anti-nuclear arms	pro-choice
ex-President	post-World War II
mid-March	

PUNCTUATION

✔ Use a hyphen for a compound adjective when it comes before the noun it modifies.

> **worst-case** scenario
> **eye-catching** newsletter
> **bottom-line** results
> **long-range** plans
> **high-level** meeting
> **high-pressure** environment

💣 **Caution:** Do not use a hyphen after an adverb ending in *ly*, even when it is part of a compound adjective that precedes a noun. Readers expect such words to modify the word that follows; therefore, the hyphen is implied and not necessary.

> highly valued employee
> newly formed division
> clearly defined business goals

✔ Use a hyphen for two nouns that refer to one person or when one thing has two functions.

> owner-manager
> clerk-typist
> secretary-treasurer
> dinner-dance

✔ Use a hyphen for many compound nouns that have a single letter as their first element.

T-shirt	A-frame
U-turn	H-bomb

✔ Use a hyphen when a number and a noun form a compound modifier before another noun.

2-liter bottle	20-year mortgage
100-meter dash	50-cent fee
8-foot ceiling	

PUNCTUATION

✔ Use a hyphen for compound adjectives involving a number and *odd* or *plus*.

30-plus members	20-odd years ago

✔ Use a hyphen for a compound adjective composed of one noun and one adjective.

bone-dry	cost-effective
letter-perfect	ice-cold
machine-readable	tax-exempt
sky-high	street-smart
top-heavy	year-round

🖊 **Note:** Use a hyphen when writing out numbers from twenty-one through ninety-nine. Do not hyphenate hundreds, thousands, or millions.

Ellipses points   . . .

Ellipses points are a series of spaced periods that show omission of an idea or an idea that trails off.

✎**Rules:**

✔ Three spaced periods can be used at the beginning or in the middle of a quoted sentence to show an omitted idea.

✔ If an omitted idea appears at the end of a sentence, a fourth dot should be used to represent the final period.

> ". . . Whether 'tis nobler . . . to suffer the slings and arrows of outrageous fortune."
>
> ". . . Whether 'tis nobler in the mind to suffer . . . ."

PUNCTUATION

Apostrophes   '

An apostrophe is a mark used to indicate absent letters in contractions, dialect, and the possessive case.

✑Rules:

✔ Use an apostrophe in the place of letters or numbers that have been left out.

Class of '73	aren't
gov't	we're

✔ Use an apostrophe to create a possessive form of a noun.

> Susan's report
> Phoenix's zoo
> students' scores

✔ Use an apostrophe to form a plural of a word or letter that otherwise would be misread.

> or's and nor's
> a's and i's

💣 **Caution:** To pluralize numbers expressed in figures, add an *s* without an apostrophe.

Incorrect:
> 1990's

Correct:

> 1990s

PLURALS AND POSSESSIVES

The plural form of most nouns is usually represented by adding s *or* es *to the singular.*

The possessive case is used to indicate a relationship of possession. A possessive pronoun is a word that attributes ownership to someone or something without using a noun.

Plurals

🖋 **Rules:**

✔ The most common ending for a plural is an *s* added to the singular.

report	reports
committee	committees
manager	managers
idea	ideas

✔ Some nouns have a word ending that would make the s difficult or impossible to pronounce. Nouns ending in *s*, *x*, *ch*, *sh*, or *z* generally require an *es* added to the singular.

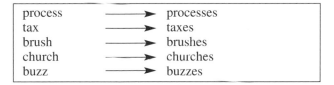

process	processes
tax	taxes
brush	brushes
church	churches
buzz	buzzes

✔ Nouns ending in *y* have two possibilities.

➤ If the singular noun ends in *y* preceded by a consonant, change the *y* to *i* and add *es*.

copy	copies
disability	disabilities
liability	liabilities

➤ If the singular noun ends in *y* preceded by a vowel, simply add *s*.

attorney	attorneys
delay	delays
boy	boys

PLURALS AND POSSESSIVES

✔ The plurals for nouns ending in *o* can be formed in two ways.

➤ If the singular noun ends in *o* preceded by a vowel, add *s*.

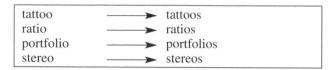

tattoo	⟶ tattoos
ratio	⟶ ratios
portfolio	⟶ portfolios
stereo	⟶ stereos

➤ However, if the singular noun ends in *o* preceded by a consonant, there are several possibilities.

Some *o* nouns add only an *s*.

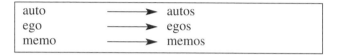

auto	⟶ autos
ego	⟶ egos
memo	⟶ memos

Some *o* nouns add *es*.

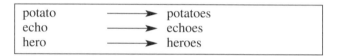

potato	⟶ potatoes
echo	⟶ echoes
hero	⟶ heroes

Some *o* nouns are acceptable either way. The first in each pair is the preferred spelling.

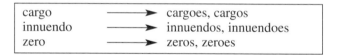

cargo	⟶ cargoes, cargos
innuendo	⟶ innuendos, innuendoes
zero	⟶ zeros, zeroes

Musical terms ending in *o* usually add only *s* to the singular.

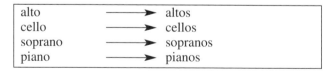

alto	⟶ altos
cello	⟶ cellos
soprano	⟶ sopranos
piano	⟶ pianos

PLURALS AND POSSESSIVES

✔ Nouns ending in *f*, *fe*, or *ff*.

➤ Most nouns ending in *f* combinations add only *s* to the singular.

belief	➤	beliefs
proof	➤	proofs

➤ Some *f* nouns change the *f* or *fe* to *ve* and then add *s*.

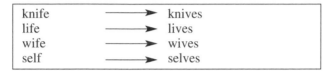

knife	➤	knives
life	➤	lives
wife	➤	wives
self	➤	selves

➤ Some are acceptable either way. Again, the first in each pair is the preferred spelling.

scarf	➤	scarves, scarfs
dwarf	➤	dwarfs, dwarves

✔ Compound plurals are made plural by using several methods.

➤ Solid-word compounds are made plural at the end.

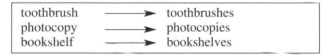

toothbrush	➤	toothbrushes
photocopy	➤	photocopies
bookshelf	➤	bookshelves

➤ Compounds that are spaced or hyphenated generally make the most important element plural.

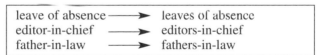

leave of absence	➤	leaves of absence
editor-in-chief	➤	editors-in-chief
father-in-law	➤	fathers-in-law

💣 **Caution:** I have two sisters-in-law, not two sister-in-laws. But, I went to my sister-in-law's house for Thanksgiving.

➤ Compounds with no noun simply make the final element plural.

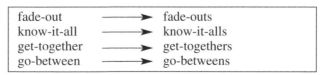

fade-out	➤	fade-outs
know-it-all	➤	know-it-alls
get-together	➤	get-togethers
go-between	➤	go-betweens

PLURALS AND POSSESSIVES

➤ Compounds that have a possessive as the first element make only the final element plural.

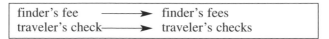

finder's fee	⟶	finder's fees
traveler's check	⟶	traveler's checks

➤ Acronyms and capital letters require only an *s* to create the plural.

three VIPs	CEOs	Ph.D.s	PTAs

➤ Irregular plurals change their spelling completely.

mouse	⟶	mice
woman	⟶	women
foot	⟶	feet

➤ A few plurals end in *en* or *ren*.

ox	⟶	oxen
child	⟶	children

Singular nouns and possession

🖎 **Rules:**

✔ Any singular noun not ending in *s* or an *s* sound adds an apostrophe plus *s*.

> lawyer's advice
>
> Arkansas's farmlands
>
> Illinois's toll roads

✔ Any singular noun that ends in the sound *s*, *x*, or *z* is affected by how it's pronounced.

➤ If you add an extra syllable, add an apostrophe plus *s*.

> boss's approval
>
> witness's testimony
>
> quiz's coversheet
>
> Phoenix's transportation system

PLURALS AND POSSESSIVES

> ➤ If you cannot easily pronounce the word with an additional syllable, add only an apostrophe.

> Ms. Hastings' office
>
> Los Angeles' freeways
>
> New Orleans' shopping district

💣 **Caution:** It's *Bridget **Jones'** Diary*, not *Bridget **Jones's** Diary*.

Plural nouns and possession

✎ **Rules:**

✔ Any plural noun with a regular spelling (ending in *s* or *es*) adds only an apostrophe for possession.

> witnesses' testimonies
>
> agencies' guidelines
>
> United States' allies
>
> attorneys' fees

✔ All irregular plural possessives add an apostrophe plus *s*.

> children's books
>
> men's suits
>
> women's dress department

💣 **Caution:** Always form the plural first and then decide how the possession should be spelled.

Incorrect:

> Toys are located in the childrens' department.

Correct:

> Toys are located in the children's department.

PLURALS AND POSSESSIVES

Compound nouns and possession

🔖 **Rules:**

✔ Singular possessives of any compound noun (solid, spaced, or hyphenated) require an apostrophe plus *s*.

> stockbroker's portfolio
>
> daughter-in-law's new house
>
> attorney general's office

✔ Plural possessives for compound nouns require you to first form the plural, then:

➤ If the plural form ends in *s*, add an apostrophe only.

> stockbrokers' proxies
>
> vice presidents' votes
>
> salesclerks' commissions

➤ If the plural form does not end in *s*, add an apostrophe plus *s*.

> daughters-in-law's children
>
> presidents-elect's teams

🖝 **See also**: Apostrophes, *Punctuation* section

✔ Pronouns have their own special forms. Do not use apostrophes!

my, mine	your, yours	his, her, hers, its
our, ours	their, theirs	whose

PLURALS AND POSSESSIVES

💣 **Caution:** *Whose* is a pronoun, while *who's* is a contraction for "who is."

Incorrect:

> He is the man who's son goes to K-State.

Correct:

He is the man whose son goes to K-State.

👓 **See also**: Pronouns, *Sentence Construction* section

✔ Common expressions

New Year's resolutions
stone's throw
arm's length
sun's rays
company's assets
earth's atmosphere

TITLES AND CAPITALIZATION

Capitalization custom varies with language. The full rules of capitalization for English are complicated and have changed over time, generally to capitalize fewer terms.

Titles

☜ Rules:

✔ Capitalize all official titles of honor and respect when they precede personal names.

> *Courtesy titles:*
> Mr., Mrs., Ms., Miss
> *Executive titles:*
> President, Vice President, Director
> *Professional titles:*
> Professor, Dr.
> *Civic titles:*
> Governor, Senator, Ambassador, Mayor
> *Military titles:*
> Colonel, Captain, Commander, Lieutenant
> *Religious titles:*
> Rabbi, Reverend, Father

&⌐ **See also**: Colons, *Punctuation* section

In general, do *not* capitalize a title if:

1. It is set off by commas from the personal name that follows.

2. It is an occupational title such as author, drama critic, etc.

3. It follows the name, or is used in place of the name.

4. It identifies a lesser federal or state official.

5. It stands alone.

6. It is a general term of classification.

TITLES AND CAPITALIZATION

Job titles

✎**Rules:**

✔ Capitalize titles that replace the names of high-ranking national, state, and international officials.

> The Prime Minister visited Washington, D.C.,
> last week.

✔ Titles of company officials (president, general manager) should not be capitalized when they follow or replace a personal name. Exceptions are made for formal minutes of meetings. Some companies choose to capitalize titles in all organizational communications out of respect for the management.

> Mike Jones, chief risk officer, held a meeting
> last week with Laurie Miller, general manager.

✔ Capitalize any job title in formal citations and acknowledgments.

✔ Capitalize any title used in direct address (i.e., communication directly to another person).

> Dear President Johnson,

✔ Capitalize all titles preceding or following a name: on an envelope, in the inside address of a letter, or in a writer's identification block.

> Joe Wilkinson, Assistant Vice President
> 3700 College Boulevard
> Overland Park, KS 66214

💣 **Caution:** Do not capitalize job titles that stand alone, unless they require special emphasis in procedure manuals or company memos and announcements.

💣 **Caution:** Do not capitalize *former, late, ex,* or *-elect* when used with a title.

> the late President Truman
> ex-President Clinton

⤷ **See also**: Capitalization, *Quick Reference* section

TITLES AND CAPITALIZATION

Particular vs. general names

✎ **Rules:**

✔ Capitalize specific names of places such as streets, buildings, parks, monuments, rivers, oceans, and mountains, but not general terms.

Red Mountain	the mountain
Times Square	the square
Salt River	the river
Stapleton Airport	the airport
Lake Como	the lake
Stone Mountain Park	the park

🖉 **Note:** Some places have become so closely associated with one thing that they are always capitalized, even without the name.

the Coast	(East Coast)
the Hill	(Capitol Hill)
the Channel	(English Channel)

✔ Capitalize words such as *mother, father, aunt, uncle*, etc., when they stand alone or are followed by a personal name. Do not capitalize family titles preceded by possessives such as *my, your, our, her*, or *his* when they describe a family relationship.

my aunt	Aunt Theresa

✔ Common organizational terms for internal departments, divisions, etc. are capitalized in the business writer's **own company**, but are not typically capitalized when they refer to someone else's organization.

marketing	advertising
accounting	

✔ Capitalize words such as *northern, southern, eastern*, and *western* when they refer to the people in a region or to their political, social, or cultural activities.

Southern hospitality
southern scenery
Eastern schools
eastern half of New York
Southerner
Northerner

TITLES AND CAPITALIZATION

💣 **Caution:** Be sure to carefully review rules of capitalization.

Incorrect:

> I visited family in Western Kansas for the holidays.

Correct:

> I visited family in the western part of Kansas for the holidays.

Quotations

✍ **Rules:**

✔ Capitalize the first word of a quoted complete sentence.

> He said, "This will be the best quarter ever!"

✔ In a quoted word or phrase, capitalize the first word only if:

➤ It is a proper noun, proper adjective, or the pronoun *I*.

> The one thing people notice immediately about her is her "Southern drawl."

➤ It was capitalized in the original use.

> He jotted "Approved" on the bottom of Linda's vacation request, and then signed it.

➤ It is at the beginning of a sentence.

> "Ridiculous" was the term the board members used in reaction to the negative sales predictions.

👓 **See also:** Quotation marks, **Punctuation** section

TITLES AND CAPITALIZATION

Languages, races, and nationalities

Rules:

✔ Capitalize the names of races, tribes, and languages.

Native Americans	Hispanics
African Americans	Caucasians

Note: Hyphenate double words used as adjectives.

African-American studies
French-Canadian voters

ELECTRONIC MAIL

Many business people throw formality to the wind when writing e-mail, but remember that "businesslike" means respectful. Show your reader some respect by putting thought into your e-mail creations. It can take hours to wade through the daily e-mail. Save your reader some time with the following tips.

✔ Distribute sparingly. Send only to those who truly need to know.

✔ Keep messages—shorter than memos and far shorter than letters.

✔ Refer to previous e-mails to orient your reader.

✔ Write a to-the-point subject line. This lets the reader decide whether to read it now or save it for later. Keep it short, and use action verbs to get people's attention.

✔ Keep to one subject.

✔ Watch your tone.

✔ Avoid emoticons (keyboard characters that represent facial expressions or emotions).

✔ Use the salutation you would use in a letter.

✔ Use the complementary close you would use in a letter.

✔ Sign your name, title, company name, address, e-mail address, and fax and voice numbers.

✔ Use proper punctuation and capitalization.

✔ Avoid using all capitals.

Help Your Reader:

☐ For in-house e-mails that take the place of paper memos, you may use company jargon and technical terminology, but always use the clearest language possible.

☐ Organize into levels. Use headings and subheadings to steer your reader. Use bullets and daggers to show levels of depth.

☐ Keep paragraphs short and always put your purpose up front.

☐ Keep in mind that "all caps" are the written equivalent of shouting, and should be used only for extreme emphasis. Use italics for emphasis and boldface to catch the eye but, remember, some people receive e-mail in plain text only. If your message isn't clear without added formatting, rewrite it.

QUICK REFERENCE

Transitions—*Use these words to connect ideas:*	
addition	again, also, and, and then, besides, beyond, equally important, finally, first, further, furthermore, in addition, in the first place, last, moreover, next, second, still, too
cause/effect	as a result of, because of, consequently, due to, leading to, thus, therefore
comparison	also, in the same way, likewise, similarly
concession	granted, naturally, of course
contrast	although, and yet, at the same time, but at the same time, despite that, even so, even though, for all that, however, in contrast, in spite of, instead, nevertheless, notwithstanding, on the contrary, on the other hand, otherwise, regardless, still, though, yet
emotion or value judgment	extremely, fortunately, spectacularly, unfortunately
emphasis	certainly, indeed, in fact, of course
example or illustration	after all, as an illustration, even, for example, for instance, in conclusion, indeed, in fact, in other words, in short, it is true, of course, namely, specifically, that is, to illustrate, thus, truly
frequency	always, annually, daily, every day, frequently, monthly, never, often, regularly, seldom, sometimes
movement	above, backing away from, just beyond, further along, toward
summary	all in all, altogether, as has been said, finally, in brief, in conclusion, in other words, in particular, in short, in simpler terms, in summary, on the whole, that is, therefore, to put it differently, to sum up, to summarize
time sequence	after a while, afterward, again, also, and then, as long as, at last, at length, at that time, before, besides, earlier, eventually, finally, formerly, further, furthermore, in addition, in the first place, in the past, last, lately, meanwhile, moreover, next, now, presently, second, shortly, simultaneously, since, so far, soon, still, subsequently, then, thereafter, too, until, until now, when

QUICK REFERENCE

Capitalization—*Capitalize the following:*	
Salutation in a letter	**Dear** Mrs. Hinton:
Closing in a letter	**Sincerely,**
Adjectives derived from proper nouns	**Norwegian** (Norway)
Imaginative nicknames	**Founding Fathers** **Stars and Stripes**
Companies, unions, associations, societies, committees, boards, political parties, conventions, fraternities, sororities, clubs, religious bodies	**Parents Anonymous** **Democratic Party** **Sigma Chi Fraternity** **Retail Clerks Union**
Countries; international organizations; national, state, county, and city bodies	**British Commonwealth** **House of Representatives** **Hartford City Council**
Short forms of national and international bodies	the **House** (House of Representatives) the **Bureau** (Federal Bureau of Investigation)
Imaginative place names	the **Big Apple** the **French Quarter**
Days	**Wednesday, Friday**
Months	**June, August**
Holidays	**Halloween, Fourth of July**
Religious holy days	**Easter, Yom Kippur, Ramadan**
Historic events	**World War II**
Historic periods	the **Great Depression**
Cultural ages	the **Dark Ages**
Cultural eras	the **Victorian Era**
Decades (in special expressions)	the **Roaring Twenties**
Acts, laws, bills, treaties	**Treaty of Versailles** **Public Law 714** **Constitution of the United States**

QUICK REFERENCE

Capitalization—*Capitalize the following:*	
Laws, rules or objects named for people or mythical figures.	**Murphy's Law, Boyle's Law, Sword of Damocles, Occam's Razor**
Imaginative names of programs, movements	**New Deal**
Adjectives describing a concept, movement	**Socratic method Newtonian physics**
Membership in a political party	A lifelong **Socialist**
Sacred works	**Koran, Torah,** the **Ten Commandments**
References to supreme beings	The **Messiah, Allah, God**
Names of religions, their members and specific places of workship	**Mormons, Methodists, Roman Catholics, Judaism, Notre Dame Cathedral**
Planets, stars, constellations	**Saturn, Alpha Centauri, Ursa Major**
Course titles	**American History 101**
Academic degree after a person's name	**Ellen Smith, M.A.**
Trademarks, brands, proprietary names, commercial products	**Velcro, Band-Aid, Tylenol, Dixie Cup, Popsicle, Frigidaire, Monopoly**
Nouns followed by a number or letter	**Flight 1104, Appendix B, Chapter 4, Room 105, Policy 743921, Invoice 1601**
Awards, medals	**Oscar, Emmy, Nobel Prize, Purple Heart**
Computer operating systems	**MS-DOS, Windows, Unix**
Software applications	**DisplayWrite, WordPerfect, PageMaker**
Towers, monuments,and buildings	**The Eiffel Tower, The Washington Monument, The Empire State Building**

QUICK REFERENCE

Numbers—*Write these numbers as words:*	
Any number below 10	**Three, five, eight**
An indefinite number	A **hundred** things to do
Exact or approximate numbers expressed as one or two words	More than **two hundred** people
Dates in formal legal documents, formal invitations, and proclamations	This **seventeenth** day of March
Indefinite amounts of money	Many **thousands** of dollars
Numbers beginning sentences	**Nine hundred** people have already signed the petition.
Ordinal numbers that can be expressed in one or two words	**Forty-third** birthday *43rd* **Twenty-first** century *21st*
Fractions standing alone without a whole number	**Two-thirds** majority *2/3*
Ages in nontechnical reference or formal writing	Her son is **three** years old.
Ordinal numbers in reference to birthdays and anniversaries	My **thirtieth** anniversary *13th*
The smaller of two numbers that are part of a compound modifier (a two-part adjective)	**Four 32-cent** stamps
Street numbers below 10, or the number "One"	**Fourth** Avenue **One** Main Street
Clock time used before the word "o'clock" or standing alone	He left at **five o'clock**. Stop by at **eleven**.
The word "cents" for any amount below a dollar (rather than the symbol)	**25 cents**
All numbers 10 and above	**12, 18, 600**
Large numbers such as million or billion	**24** million
A date where the day follows the month	April **6**

QUICK REFERENCE

Numbers—*Write these numbers as numerals:*

Approximate amounts of money	Nearly **$50,000**
Numbered streets 10 and above	**18th** Street
A mixed number (whole number plus a fraction, unless it appears at the beginning of a sentence)	Sales are **3 1/2** times greater than last year.
Technical measurements	**1** pint, **2** quarts, **25**-mile radius
Dimensions, sizes, weight	**4 x 6**, shirt size **17/34**, **150** pounds
Temperature readings	**35** degrees
Ages	**18** to **35** age group
Interest rates, credit terms	**30**-year mortgage
Clock time using a.m., p.m., noon, and midnight	**4:45** p.m., **12** noon
Percentages (write the word percent)	**15** percent
Ratios and proportions	**5:1** ratio
Scores, voting results	Seattle **101**, Chicago **98** A vote of **15** to **7**
Abbreviations, symbols	**150** km, **72** c
Ordinal numbers that cannot be expressed in one or two words	She is the **150**th person to attend the sale.
Decimals	**72.019**
Amounts of money	A **$20** bill

EXERCISES IN GRAMMAR

Exercise 1 – Parallelism

Rewrite these sentences that have faulty parallelism in a form that reflects consistent grammatical construction. Express parallel ideas in parallel form.

1. There is a market for stylish mobile communication among the French, the Italians, Spanish, and Portuguese.

2. It was both a long meeting and very productive.

3. Either you must file his request or act on it now.

4. The new accounts director has experience, dedication, and she has an extremely professional demeanor.

5. The national office rewarded Region Three for its high sales and going beyond the call of duty.

6. Antonio's motivation to succeed in this position seems to be greater than his predecessor.

7. I have no doubt about your care and interest in the project.

division of PARK University Enterprises, Inc.

www.careertrack.com

EXERCISES IN GRAMMAR

Exercise 2 – Pronouns: Reflexive, Subject/Object

Choose the correct word to finish each of the following sentences.

1. Kai, Chandra, and _____(I, me, myself) are headed to the conference now.

2. Give the paperwork to _____(she, her, herself) so that it can be submitted this pay period.

3. Edward stayed all weekend to finish that report all by _____ (he, him, himself).

4. Anders gave a copy of that memo to Jim, Tom, and _____ (I, me, myself).

5. To _____(who, whom) should the packages be addressed?

6. The company's analysts _____(they, their, themselves) knew what _____(they, them, their) predictions were based on, but no one else understood_____(them, their, themselves).

7. Just between you and_____(I, me), I think this is the best work we've ever done.

8. Jonquil wondered why _____(she, her) employees complained about a lack of vacation since _____(she, her) _____ (hers, herself) never took a day off.

CAREERTRACK.

division of PARK University Enterprises, Inc.

www.careertrack.com

EXERCISES IN GRAMMAR

Exercise 3 – Subjects and Verbs

Choose the correct word(s) to finish each of the following sentences.

1. Maggie, along with Jack and Jose, _____(is, are) meeting Bob and Hilda at the restaurant.

2. Everyone _____(know, knows) the outcome of the vote.

3. That dog is _____(your's, yours).

4. Either of the two choices _____(is, are) fine.

5. If I _____ (was, were) to go, I would need to pack my laptop.

6. Sara, as well as several other employees, _____ (is, are) familiar with the policy.

7. I _____ (shall, will) call Mrs. King tomorrow.

8. _____ (Its, It's) good vendor management to hold the supplier accountable.

9. The reasons for the problem _____ (was, were) too numerous.

10. The group _____ (have, has) left the conference room.

division of PARK University Enterprises, Inc.

www.careertrack.com

EXERCISES IN GRAMMAR

Exercise 4 – Verb Tenses

What verb tenses are the bold portions of these sentences in? Write the correct tense for each of the following.

1. I **had already spent** the money for the copy machine when I remembered that we needed a new desk. _____

2. You **will find** that the atmosphere here is incredibly welcoming to recent college graduates. _____

3. Vita **is looking** for a new hobby, since her old hobby became a multi-million dollar business. _____

4. When the clock strikes 5:30, I **will have been** here for over twenty-four hours. _____

5. Charles **has waited** for an hour to talk to Annika, but she is still occupied in a closed-door meeting. _____

6. I **spoke** to Human Resources about the lack of soap in the bathrooms, but it did not do much good. _____

7. Each year, without fail, Felipe **reviews** the performance of every employee in February. _____

8. Upper management **will have made** a decision about next year's budget before we meet again to discuss our departmental plans. _____

9. We **have found** that the best method of recycling paper is to reuse the blank side as scratch paper. _____

10. Alva **had recruited** 15 clients for the business before we realized that he doesn't always present our services accurately. _____

EXERCISES IN GRAMMAR

Exercise 5 – Adjectives and Adverbs

Adjective or adverb form? Circle the correct answer for each of the following.

1. It was a (real, really) dull convention.

2. Bart manages people (good, well).

3. Bart is a (good, well) manager.

4. You did a (remarkable, remarkably) job.

5. He finished the project (satisfactorily, satisfactory).

6. Remove the cap very (slow, slowly) to avoid being burned by the hot steam.

7. Tom was embarrassed because they performed (bad, badly).

8. He must act (quick, quickly) to take advantage of the discount.

9. Send the contract (immediate, immediately) to get the best price.

10. The production manager is (real, really) pleased with the current production levels.

EXERCISES IN GRAMMAR

Exercise 6 – Prepositions and Conjunctions

Is the boldfaced word a preposition or conjunction? Circle the correct response.

1. Gerald hopes his monkey will jump **over** the fence.
   (preposition, conjunction)

2. Angela **and** Harold are going to the meeting.
   (preposition, conjunction)

3. I knew we would be late, **but** we had to stop at the post office.
   (preposition, conjunction)

4. The file cabinet was at the back **of** the office.
   (preposition, conjunction)

5. The assistant told the salesperson not to bug her, **yet** she gave him a
   business card.
   (preposition, conjunction)

6. Julie planned to complete the project on time **and** under budget.
   (preposition, conjunction)

7. **In addition to** the paperwork, Stan needs to take his passport picture
   with him.
   (preposition, conjunction)

8. The deadline must be readjusted if she does not complete the analysis **by**
   Monday.
   (preposition, conjunction)

9. Tony excelled in his group, **so** he was promoted.
   (preposition, conjunction)

10. The mail production facility is located **behind** the conference room.
    (preposition, conjunction)

EXERCISES IN GRAMMAR

Exercise 7 – Conjunctions

Choose the proper conjunction from the list for each of the sentences below.

for   nor   yet   but   and   or   so

1. Either the desk _____ the dining room table can go in the corner of the room.

2. I would have gone to the party, _____ I lost the address of the restaurant.

3. Nate hates cake, _____ we only had ice cream at his birthday party.

4. Make the most of the day, _____ the night is long.

5. Alison was pleased with the way her life had turned out, _____ she always wondered what would have happened if she hadn't joined the circus.

6. The deluxe sandwich was tremendously expensive, _____ the standard sandwich was not cheap either.

7. I will not be in the office this Wednesday, _____ will I be here the following Thursday.

EXERCISES IN GRAMMAR

Exercise 8 – Types of Sentences

Identify the following sentences as simple, compound, complex, or compound-complex.

1. The desk is unusually shiny. _____

2. Nancy finally arrived, though she was half an hour late.
   _____

3. The boss called at 10, but she wasn't supposed to call until 11.
   _____

4. All the e-mails were sent to John; consequently, nobody knew about the problem. _____

5. Even though the CEO assured everyone all was okay, some of the employees were nervous about returning to work, and I can't blame them.
   _____

6. Most of the employees attended the morning training session.
   _____

7. Stan can speak Spanish, and Susan speaks French.
   _____

8. The shipment arrived in the warehouse, although the warehouse staff was not ready to receive the delivery. _____

9. Sales in September were better than expected, but the increased revenue did not offset last month's losses. _____

10. He finished the report last night. _____

CAREERTRACK.

division of PARK University Enterprises, Inc.

www.careertrack.com

EXERCISES IN GRAMMAR

Exercise 9 – Creating Types of Sentences

1. For each phrase below, identify the correct phrase type.

   the era of computers is coming to a close (independent/dependent)
   new technology will take the place of
   the almighty computer (independent/dependent)

2. Using the phrases above, create a compound sentence with a semicolon.

   _____

   _____

3. Using the same phrases, create a compound sentence with a conjunction.

   _____

   _____

4. For each phrase below, identify the correct phrase type.

   when the sun sinks below the horizon (independent/dependent)
   pink tendrils cling to the clouds (independent/dependent)
   for as long as they can (independent/dependent)

5. Using the phrases above, create a complex sentence.

   _____

   _____

EXERCISES IN GRAMMAR

Exercise 10 – Active Voice vs. Passive Voice

Determine if sentences are active or passive. Circle the correct response. Try rewriting the passive sentences to make them active.

1. The manuals were written by Alex in Accounting.
    (active/passive)

2. When you are done with the ruler, please return it to Marco.
    (active/passive)

3. Before the trip to Acapulco can be approved by management, we will have to access the accounts saved by Midge.
    (active/passive)

4. When you go to the Main Street office, will you take this envelope?
    (active/passive)

5. A study was conducted by executive management to determine if damage to the coffee machine was done by employees.
    (active/passive)

EXERCISES IN GRAMMAR

Exercise 11 – Subjunctive Voice

Rewrite the following sentences using the correct subjunctive voice.

1. If I was any taller, I would hit my head on the door frame whenever I walk into the room.

2. I insist that you are considerate of the feelings of everyone in the room.

3. If stores in town would stock enough molasses, I would not drive to the next county for it.

4. I wish I was in Oklahoma with my family this week.

5. I would buy you a stable for your unicorn if you would prove that the creature actually exists.

EXERCISES IN GRAMMAR

Exercise 12 – Sentence Structure 1

What is wrong with the following sentences? Write your answers in the blank spaces below.

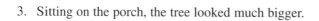

1. Mark, Vince, Margaret, and myself went to Zippo's for lunch.

2. I asked Jimmy what the problem was, but he didn't say nothing.

3. Sitting on the porch, the tree looked much bigger.

4. The project was completed by Laura.

5. Call Doug and me when you get back.

EXERCISES IN GRAMMAR

Exercise 13 – Sentence Structure 2

What is wrong with the following sentences? Write your answers in the blank spaces below.

1. Something ought to be done about the rapid increasing number of lunch containers in the refrigerator.

2. On Garrick's first day as managing editor, the phone rung relentlessly.

3. I like convertibles which are red and incredibly fast.

4. According to many top-ranked athletes, neither the crowd's cheers nor the money are more important than the satisfaction of competing well.

5. The volunteers which were to help us staple booklets left after two hours.

division of PARK University Enterprises, Inc.

www.careertrack.com

EXERCISES IN GRAMMAR

Exercise 14 – Spelling

Correct the following misspelled words.

1. Financeal

2. Argueing

3. Enforcable

4. Hopefull

5. Mimicced

6. Franchize

7. Analize

8. Defendent

9. Dependible

10. Occuring

EXERCISES IN GRAMMAR

Exercise 15 – Usage 1

Circle the correct choice to complete each of the following sentences.

1. It doesn't (affect/effect) me either way.

2. Georgia (eluded, alluded) to the conversation we had earlier.

3. I took him to the (sight/cite/site) of the new building.

4. I think the black really (compliments/complements) the red.

5. We asked Geoff's opinion since he is a(n) (disinterested/uninterested) bystander.

6. Jinx says she wants to go (to/too).

7. From Johnson's attitude, I (implied/inferred) there was trouble.

8. It's the (principle/principal) of the thing that makes me question his integrity.

9. I said my goodbyes (respectively/respectfully) to avoid hard feelings.

10. His book is better (then, than) hers.

EXERCISES IN GRAMMAR

Exercise 16 – Usage 2

Circle the correct choice to complete each of the following sentences.

1. The heroine saved millions of lives, but nearly lost her own, in the most (climatic/climactic) moment of the movie.

2. Sean told a joke to (defuse/diffuse) the hostile tension that developed amongst the guests.

3. We will (precede/proceed) with the demolition once the residents have removed their belongings.

4. A professional arbiter acts as a(n) (uninterested/disinterested) party to help resolve a dispute.

5. I have a (veracious/voracious) thirst for knowledge about medieval financial institutions, a passionate interest of mine.

6. Our goal of becoming the top firm in the industry was (elusive/illusive) until Sandro joined the company.

7. Are you trying to (imply/infer) that I had ulterior motives in choosing my sister's company for the contract?

8. I don't like speaking to her because she seems to (critique/criticize) something about me every time she opens her mouth.

9. We are out of time for now, but we can discuss this (farther/further) at a later date.

10. Health insurance will be (deducted/deduced) from your salary before taxes are calculated.

division of PARK University Enterprises, Inc.

www.careertrack.com

EXERCISES IN GRAMMAR

Exercise 17 – Punctuation 1

Punctuate the following sentences correctly.

1. I asked Donna to get the report to me Monday however she did not get it to me until Wednesday

2. Linus asked for pens pencils and erasers for the meeting

3. Program Assistant Program Manager and Program Director those were the positions she held here

4. Jennys response was The last one was yours

5. Dr Smith gave us only nine flu shots therefore we will have to give them out on a first come first served basis

division of PARK University Enterprises, Inc.

www.careertrack.com

EXERCISES IN GRAMMAR

Exercise 18 – Punctuation 2

Punctuate the following sentences correctly.

1. If you are worried about getting injured stand back this blade is very sharp

2. I dont believe all her friends should call her doctor just because she received a PhD

3. The list of magazines for which she models is bizarre *Motorweek Scientific American and Knitters Digest*

4. The trained chimpanzee wearing a striped shirt and a beanie no less strolled down the street making balloon animals

5. In the absence of a better suggestion we will adjourn this meeting for it is better to come back to these ideas with a fresh mind tomorrow said the judge

EXERCISES IN GRAMMAR

Exercise 19 – Plurals and Possessives

Write the possessive forms of the following words.

1. boss assistant (one boss)

2. bosses assistants (several bosses)

3. mother-in-law house

4. people coats (coats of several people)

5. manager report (one manager)

6. managers reports (several managers)

EXERCISES IN GRAMMAR

Exercise 20 – Transitions

Match up each transition from the list with the appropriate sentence.

a. however   b. furthermore   c. therefore   d. in addition

e. despite   f. while   g. another

1. We have three new lines of clothing ready to unveil this spring. _____, we are developing a line of shoes that complement the fashions.

2. _____ example of this kind of flagrant disregard of company policy is your refusal to come in before noon.

3. _____ beneficial to some, the office's change of location means that some face a longer commute.

4. It is almost the end of the quarter, _____, we need to finalize the text for the quarterly report.

5. _____ a formerly strong rivalry between the companies, they successfully brokered a merger.

6. We finished the first round of interviews; _____, there is much to do before we narrow the candidates to a reasonable number of applicants.

7. _____ to the preparations that we have already confirmed, we must double-check that the caterer will bring the coffee urns that we requested.

CAREERTRACK.
division of PARK University Enterprises, Inc.

www.careertrack.com

ANSWERS TO EXERCISES 1-20

Exercise 1 – Parallelism

1. There is a market for stylish mobile communication among the French, the Italians, the Spanish, and the Portuguese.
2. The meeting was both long and productive.
3. You must either file his request or act on it now.
4. The new accounts director has experience, dedication, and a professional demeanor.
5. The national office rewarded Region Three for selling the highest volume and going beyond the call of duty.
6. Antonio's motivation to succeed in this position seems to be greater than his predecessor's.
7. I have no doubt about your care for and interest in the project.

Exercise 2 – Pronouns: Reflexive, Subject/Object

1. I
2. her
3. himself
4. me
5. whom
6. themselves, their, them
7. me
8. her, she, herself

Exercise 3 – Subjects and Verbs

1. is
2. knows
3. yours
4. is
5. were
6. is
7. will
8. It's
9. were
10. has

Exercise 4 – Verb Tenses

1. past perfect
2. simple future
3. simple present
4. future perfect
5. present perfect
6. simple past
7. simple present
8. future perfect
9. present perfect
10. past perfect

Exercise 5 – Adjectives and Adverbs

1. really
2. well
3. good
4. remarkable
5. satisfactorily
6. slowly
7. badly
8. quickly
9. immediately
10. really

ANSWERS TO EXERCISES 1-20

Exercise 6 – Prepositions and Conjunctions

1. preposition
2. conjunction
3. conjunction
4. preposition
5. conjunction
6. conjunction
7. preposition
8. preposition
9. conjunction
10. preposition

Exercise 7 – Conjunctions

1. or
2. but
3. so
4. for
5. yet (or but)
6. and
7. nor

Exercise 8 – Types of Sentences

1. simple
2. complex
3. compound
4. compound
5. compound-complex
6. simple
7. compound
8. complex
9. compound
10. simple

Exercise 9 – Creating Types of Sentences

1. Independent.
   Independent.
2. The era of computers is coming to a close; new technology will take the place of the almighty computer.
3. The era of computers is coming to a close, but new technology will take the place of the almighty computer.
4. Dependent.
   Independent.
   Dependent.
5. When the sun sinks below the horizon, pink tendrils cling to the clouds for as long as they can.

Exercise 10 – Active Voice vs. Passive Voice

1. Passive—Possible active version: Alex in Accounting wrote the manuals.
2. Active.
3. Passive—Possible active version: Before management can approve the trip to Acapulco, we have to access the accounts Midge saved.
4. Active.
5. Passive—Possible active version: Executive management conducted a study to determine if employees damaged the coffee machine.

CAREERTRACK.

division of PARK University Enterprises, Inc.

www.careertrack.com

ANSWERS TO EXERCISES 1-20

Exercise 11 – Subjunctive Voice

1. If I were any taller, I would hit my head on the door frame whenever I walk into the room.
2. I insist that you be considerate of the feelings of everyone in the room.
3. If stores in town stocked enough molasses, I would not drive to the next county for it.
   or
   If stores in town were to stock enough molasses, I would not drive to the next county for it.
4. I wish I were in Oklahoma with my family this week.
5. I would buy you a stable for your unicorn if you were to prove that the creature actually exists.
   or
   I would buy you a stable for your unicorn if you proved that the creature actually exists.

Exercise 12 – Sentence Structure 1

1. Incorrect reflexive
2. Double negative
3. Dangling modifier
4. Passive voice
5. Nothing is wrong

Exercise 13 – Sentence Structure 2

1. Adjective "rapid" should be adverb "rapidly."
2. Incorrect verb construction. "Rung" should be "rang."
3. "which" should be "that"
4. Incorrect subject-verb agreement: "neither . . . are" should be "neither . . . is."
5. "Which" should be "who"

Exercise 14 – Spelling

1. Financial
2. Arguing
3. Enforceable
4. Hopeful
5. Mimicked
6. Franchise
7. Analyze
8. Defendant
9. Dependable
10. Occurring

Exercise 15 – Usage 1

1. It doesn't **affect** me either way.
2. Georgia **alluded** to the conversation we had earlier.
3. I took him to the **site** of the new building.
4. I think the black really **complements** the red.
5. We asked Geoff's opinion since he is a **disinterested** bystander.
6. Jinx says she wants to go **too**.
7. From Johnson's attitude, I **inferred** there was trouble.
8. It's the **principle** of the thing that makes me question his integrity.
9. I said my goodbyes **respectfully** to avoid hard feelings.
10. His book is better **than** hers.

CAREERTRACK.
division of PARK University Enterprises, Inc.

www.careertrack.com

ANSWERS TO EXERCISES 1-20

Exercise 16 – Usage 2

1. climactic
2. defuse
3. proceed
4. disinterested
5. voracious
6. elusive
7. imply
8. criticize
9. further
10. deducted

Exercise 17 – Punctuation 1

1. I asked Donna to get the report to me Monday; however, she did not get it to me until Wednesday.
2. Linus asked for pens, pencils, and erasers for the meeting.
3. Program Assistant, Program Manager, and Program Director—those were the positions she held here.
4. Jenny's response was, "The last one was yours."
5. Dr. Smith gave us only nine flu shots; therefore, we will have to give them out on a first-come-first-served basis.

Exercise 18 – Punctuation 2

1. If you are worried about getting injured, stand back; this blade is very sharp.
2. I don't believe all her friends should call her "doctor" just because she received a Ph.D.
3. The list of magazines for which she models is bizarre: *Motorweek, Scientific American*, and *Knitter's Digest.*
4. The trained chimpanzee—wearing a striped shirt and a beanie, no less—strolled down the street making balloon animals.
5. "In the absence of a better suggestion, we will adjourn this meeting, for it is better to come back to these ideas with a fresh mind tomorrow," said the judge.

Exercise 19 – Plurals and Possessives

1. boss's assistant
2. bosses' assistants
3. mother-in-law's house
4. people's coats
5. manager's report
6. managers' reports

Exercise 20 – Transitions

1. b
2. g
3. f
4. c
5. e
6. a
7. d

CAREERTRACK.

division of PARK University Enterprises, Inc.

www.careertrack.com

RECOMMENDED RESOURCES

Assertive Communication Skills for Professionals
This program will show you how to handle your communication challenges with confidence, openness, and competence. Assertive professionals exude confidence when they communicate. Using grammar correctly is an important step in gaining that confidence and communicating assertively. (Audio and video formats; published by CareerTrack)

Business Writing for Results
Whether you write memos, letters, reports, proposals, articles, performance reviews, procedure manuals, or personnel reviews—this is an excellent investment of both time and money. This program teaches the secrets of day-to-day writing in business. (Audio and video formats; published by Fred Pryor Seminars)

Evelyn Wood Memory Dynamics
What if you could remember more of the rules of grammar? This program contains tips and tricks to improve your concentration and help you remember more . . . longer. These proven methods can help you remember names, numbers, facts—anything—allowing you more time to focus on other things. (Audio format; published by Evelyn Wood)

Evelyn Wood Reading Dynamics
The most powerful weapon ever for reading faster, comprehending better, and remembering more. You'll learn how to determine your current reading rate, then increase it immediately. Your reading speed will double—guaranteed! Finish the newspaper in five or ten minutes. Rifle through magazines, reports, and trade publications in record time. Polish off entire books in one sitting. A must-have program that will enhance your professional and personal life. (Audio, video, DVD, and CD-ROM formats; published by Evelyn Wood)

Evelyn Wood Vocabulary Dynamics
People judge you by the way you speak. Using grammar correctly is important to your credibility and ability to get your point across. Combining correct grammar with a powerful vocabulary can be your greatest asset. With *Vocabulary Dynamics*, you'll learn natural vocabulary-building skills, and you'll use them to master words easily. (Audio format; published by Evelyn Wood)

High-Impact Business Writing
High-Impact Business Writing will show you how to break up big ideas, convey your thoughts clearly, and compose documents people will want to read. (Audio and video formats; published by CareerTrack)

How to Create High-Impact Letters, Memos, and E-mails
This writer's manual covers just about everything imaginable, from the writing process itself, to formatting what you've written, to checking your style. It's ideal for those moments when you need an angle, an eye-catching look, a grabber of an opener, or a good closing line and nothing comes to mind no matter how hard you search. (Spiral book; published by CareerTrack)

RECOMMENDED RESOURCES

Interpersonal Communication Skills
Experts agree that your professional success depends primarily on human-relations skills. It's not necessarily the technical skills, hard knowledge, or intelligence that make "fast-track" professionals effective in their jobs. Many times, it's superior skill in handling people that propels careers, boosts productivity, and ensures job satisfaction. (Audio and video formats; published by CareerTrack)

Mistake-Free Grammar and Proofreading for Professionals
This program demystifies the often-puzzling world of grammar, word usage, sentence structure, and punctuation. You'll gain a renewed sense of confidence in your ability to present polished, professional business communications that enhance your credibility. This audio is the perfect complement to *The Grammar Reference Guide*. (Audio format; published by CareerTrack)

The 9 Deadliest Sins of Communication
You can trace almost every workplace failure or faux pas to inadequate communication skills. The sad part is, most foul-ups could be averted if people only knew how to avoid the nine deadliest sins of communication. This skill-packed program opens your eyes to the transgressions we all commit at some time or another and offers proven, practical advice that can help you quickly correct your ways. (Video format; published by CareerTrack)

For these and other great training resources that will help you feel more confident and enhance your professional career, contact CareerTrack at 800-556-3009 or visit our Web site at careertrack.com.

INDEX

INDEX

INDEX

NOTES

NOTES

NOTES

NOTES

NOTES